planted
junk

planted
junk

RYLAND
PETERS
& SMALL
LONDON   NEW YORK

adam caplin

styling by

rose hammick

photography by

francesca yorke

For my mother

DESIGNER
Sailesh Patel

SENIOR EDITOR
Henrietta Heald

LOCATION RESEARCH MANAGER
Kate Brunt

LOCATION RESEARCHER
Sarah Hepworth

PRODUCTION
Patricia Harrington

ART DIRECTOR
Gabriella Le Grazie

PUBLISHING DIRECTOR
Alison Starling

US CONSULTANT
David Grist

INDEXER
Laura Hicks

First published in
the USA in 2001 by
Ryland Peters & Small Inc.,
519 Broadway, 5th Floor,
New York, NY 10012
www.rylandpeters.com

ISBN 1 84172 159 X
A CIP record for this
book is available from
the Library of Congress.

Printed and bound in China.

contents

the joy of junk

My first memories of junk hunting were of the times when Dad and I would leap into his old jalopy (with the top down) and zoom around to the local scrapyard. On these visits Dad introduced me to the magic of junk, and I learned to think laterally. What was a stainless steel sink to anyone else looked like a barbecue to him. In another corner of the scrapyard was the stand of an old Singer sewing machine—the perfect base for the barbecue. What's more, it worked. The makeshift barbecue was not only a good receptacle for hot charcoal, but also a great potting bench during the daylight gardening hours.

Then there were the real junk feasts: demolitions. Chimney pots, stone slabs, and metal lanterns were all among the spoils. Even our own house turned out to be full of junk opportunities. After we got bored with making our own beer, the barrel was given holes all over and planted into a complete sphere of flowers, resembling a horticultural beach ball.

As the years went by, my gardening career developed along more traditional lines as I gained experience in many aspects of horticulture, from garden maintenance to garden makeover, with the growing and retailing of plants crammed in between.

ABOVE RIGHT **A weathered galvanized bucket, an old water pump, and a fiery red abutilon combine to make an attractive junk "story" that is given clear definition by the background of a red-brick wall.**

BELOW RIGHT **Planting your junk containers can be one of the most satisfying jobs in the garden. This euphorbia had grown too large for its original pot and should settle well into its new, mobile junk home.**

Instead of fighting the existing style of your garden, you can use planted junk to enhance what is already there. The beaded basket filled with a black-leaved ophiopogon (a grass) looks great in itself and sits comfortably in the space left in front of the bamboo.

LEFT When deciding how to fill your junk pot, experiment with a variety of plants. If the planter is easy to transport, take it to your local garden center before planting, to check that the colors you are intending to put together do not clash.

Plants and junk containers sometimes seem as though they were made for each other.

My own garden was rather neglected—or, as I preferred to see it, allowed to thrive as a low-maintenance natural garden. I wanted to spend my time being creative and having fun, and finding ways to avoid mowing the lawn.

That was when planted junk really came to the fore. What could be more satisfying than to combine my love of junk hunting and exploring markets with my love of plants? The result was a yard full of beautiful plants set off by an eclectic mix of found art and junk. Often the results were startling: a wonderful complementary combination that simply looked like a natural fit. The old oval barrel from the south of France, originally used to carry grapes from the field to the winery, when planted full of hostas resembled the overflow of an abundant harvest. The olive tin stuffed full of creeping rosemary created a Mediterranean mood even on a winter's day.

At other times I lived to regret my enthusiasm, especially when it landed me with objects such as an awful jazzy 1960s vase—mercifully nudged into a pile of ugly shards by a cat with good taste.

On the day when I looked out of the window and saw that the scrapyard had taken over the backyard I realized that it had gone too far. It was time to create a more balanced effect—and now my planted junk is carefully chosen to add to the beauty of the whole. Having overreached myself in my own garden has helped me to write this book. I know the dangers of such a stimulating and potentially addictive way of gardening.

This book is written from the heart of a junk planter. It has been great fun to write, and I hope that you enjoy reading it.

BELOW, FAR LEFT **The top of this low brick wall is a perfect spot for a few junk planters. The relaxed mix of containers and plants is appropriate in the informal setting, and the planted junk on the paving stones helps to soften the horizontal and vertical lines. In a garden that is already a fusion of styles there are fewer rules than in a formal garden.**

ABOVE, FAR LEFT **The rewards of the hunt: a selection of potential junk planters wait to be assigned their new roles in the garden.**

ABOVE LEFT **A scene dominated by a long vista can work well as a stage for junk planters. The planting on this arbor walkway is so varied that it offers a wide choice of pots**

and plants, but the containers should be positioned in a such a way that they add highlights to the visual journey.

BELOW LEFT **The simple and powerful use of line and material in this modern house demands to be complemented by a simple and powerful junk planter. This galvanized metal box is an inspired choice.**

Introducing any new style to a garden can be a daunting prospect, particularly if it involves redesign and replanting—but gardening with planted junk is both easy and rewarding. A few junk containers gradually let loose among other pots, or partly hidden in a bed, can help to enhance your garden without major upheaval. The hunt for a piece of junk with planter potential—which brings an enjoyable new aspect to gardening—is a natural place to begin.

PART ONE

getting started

choosing the right pot

Placed in a bed or on a terrace or windowsill, a junk container can add to the beauty of the garden and the view—but it needs to be carefully chosen. If it grabs all the attention, upstaging everything around it, the planter is too dominant. If it is so subtle that it could be mistaken for a traditional pot, then why use it?

RIGHT Voyages of exploration to scrapyards and junk shops reveal the enormous range of potential junk containers available—from metal coal carriers and cooking pots to wooden drawers that were originally part of an old bedroom chest or dressing table.

OPPOSITE PAGE, ABOVE AND BELOW Other gems include colorful plastic buckets, wicker baskets and wirework structures of all shapes and sizes. If you approach the search for junk with an open mind, apply a generous amount of lateral thinking, and allow your imagination to roam free, the temptations are almost too numerous to mention.

Junk pots may be beautiful in themselves, and can be made even more so when planted to create a harmonious balance and positioned in such a way as to enhance the overall effect of a garden. But beware: it is easy to become carried away. Junk hunting is so much fun that the yard can become a junk muddle incorporating an eclectic mix of bizarre objects.

Whether you are simply spicing up an existing garden with a few planters or creating a more complete junk-style garden, the following guidelines will help you to identify the most appropriate junk containers for your garden

The character of your home and garden will guide you to the right pot choice.

and to create a satisfying and unique landscape. The first thing to remember is that no one starts with a completely blank canvas. Your choice of junk pot will be heavily influenced by the existing style of your home and garden, and the views.

Before visiting junk shops or starting to hunt in local dumpsters, consider how many potential junk containers are already lurking in your house or yard. Search your closets and shelves and, if you have one, your garage or cellar. You might find a discarded wine box or two, an empty paint can or even—as I did—an old crocodile teapot.

Putting a plant in an old pitcher or kettle just outside a window creates an image that becomes part of a gradual and natural transition from indoors to out—and also provides a focal point when you are in the yard looking back at the house. One of the most important features of planted junk is that the pots should sit easily within the yard and help to integrate the house and the garden.

Once you have started you will soon discover an amazing range of sources for the junk hunter, and you will eventually come to identify the best ones for the particular types of junk

When you make exciting new discoveries, it is easy to be carried away by your own enthusiasm.

you are looking for. For instance, larger pieces can often be found in stores that are being remodeled, while collecting empty cans from restaurants is not as bizarre or sad as it sounds—my local Turkish takeout place is always a good source.

If you have a distinctive view, try to work with it rather than fight it. Where there is a view of the ocean, using junk pots that have seaside connections is great fun. This approach can work well even when a garden view does not sit easily with the effect you are trying to achieve. For example, where cars or a garage form a visual barrier, an old motor-oil can overflowing with flowers can break down the barrier and create a visual poem. This is one of the keys to choosing the appropriate pot: your junk container should look like an imaginative but natural addition to your space.

Food-related junk—such as cooking equipment, old cans, and wine boxes—often forms comfortable associations with plants and sits naturally in an outdoor setting. It is as though things have come full circle: that which had been used to contain or cook food, most of which had been grown, is now itself being used to grow food or flowers.

When introducing junk to your garden, take it slowly. Live with the pots for a while before adding to them, and enjoy the organic process of design. My current favorite, a red French food can, is available only when my local deli has finished with one, so it has taken me two months to get hold of four of them.

The shared association with food means that kitchen pots and pans have an easy affinity with plants.

If you are already growing plants in containers, consider whether one or two of them could be moved into a junk pot. Some may even be crying out to get into bigger spaces. A plant that has outgrown its container informs you in various ways: roots come out of the drainage holes, the container gets dry very quickly, and the plant suffers more regularly from water stress. For advice on how to repot a potbound plant see pages 34–35.

A potted plant that you already have can determine what style of junk container you decide to use for repotting. Don't be afraid to experiment. Place the plant in various containers to see which you prefer, and try to find a pot whose color complements the plant's foliage or flowers.

OPPOSITE PAGE, ABOVE **A quick cleaning of a kitchen cabinet may turn up pots and pans that haven't seen the inside of an oven for years.**

OPPOSITE PAGE, BELOW **A toolbox and a mail-sorting rack from an office, picked up cheaply in a junk shop, wait beside a fine Icelandic poppy to be planted.**

BELOW LEFT **An old red-and-white striped can makes a stylish home for a white geranium.**

BELOW RIGHT **The green of these cans allows them to make an easy transition to junk planters.**

choosing the right pot

My garden is a fusion of styles, a mixture of tropical, formal, and natural, all living comfortably together. This gives me the freedom to use quite a diverse style of junk, although I try to establish scenes that are harmonious in themselves, grouping together similar painted cans or making a cluster of the stylish metal containers used to import olives. You are more likely to achieve a satisfactory result if you try to create one beautiful effect in a limited area rather than by being too ambitious.

If your yard has a more clearly defined style, you probably want to find junk containers to fit in with it. A formal garden with a restricted color range and geometrical patterns works best with junk that does not challenge the color tones; you can reflect the symmetry of the garden by using several of the same type of junk pot in one area. Brash plastic would be out of place, but wine boxes and strong metal shapes and wirework can produce surprisingly attractive results. A cottage-style yard with an

FAR LEFT Bamboos, tree ferns, palms, and a eucalyptus provide the dominant plant framework in this leafy yard. The Ali Baba container—originally designed to store food, drink, or oil—is now often used as a planter and adds to the tropical feel. The cordyline it contains fits into the general planting scheme.

TOP LEFT A garden with strong lines and patterns, where plants and architecture are integrated to create a coherent design, needs junk planters with similar lines to avoid breaking the pattern. These metal shopping baskets are an inspired solution. The fact that they are see-through is also valuable because a solid planter would look intimidating in such a setting.

The trick is to create one beautiful effect in a limited area.

CENTER LEFT Planted junk should be used sparingly in a modern scene dominated by man-made materials and geometrical structures. The clean lines of these pipes are in keeping with the rest of the yard, and the ivy almost appears to be a green fountain reflected in the water.

BOTTOM LEFT A restful and informal corner of the yard, distinguished by various shades of green, provides plenty of opportunities for junk planting. Choose a mixture of junk items made from natural materials in restrained colors. Plants whose beauty derives mainly from their foliage are the natural partners for such containers.

abundance of flowers and scents looks great with junk that gives the impression that it is part of the planted display, such as a wicker basket full of flowers nestling among other flowers.

In a garden that is predominantly pastel, try complementary cool colors, perhaps spiced up with a bright highlight. In a minimalist garden you can allow the dominant features to guide you. If your yard is characterized by straight lines, glass, and walls, choose junk planters with simple shapes made from modern materials—or from materials that are already dominant, such as glass. Palms, bamboos, and similar plants can be teamed with junk from exotic places to reinforce the illusion of being in a tropical country.

Don't worry if your junk planting goes wrong. It is so simple to change, and usually pretty inexpensive. However big the plant that has been put in it, an out-of-place junk planter tends to shout at you.

choosing the right plant

RIGHT **Try to create a beautiful pairing by choosing a flower color and a leaf shade that work in harmony with the junk containers. The delicate pink of these geraniums is emphasized by the cool grayish blue of the painted tin cans.**

To get the most out of your junk container, select a plant that highlights the strengths of the pot and somehow creates a balance when placed in its spot. Ultimately, this is a personal choice, and there are no hard and fast rules about how to achieve the desired effect, but there are several important factors to bear in mind when considering the options.

When choosing a plant for a junk pot, check how fast it grows. A fast-growing plant in a small container may survive if fed, watered, and pruned constantly, but it will tend to dry out quickly, become top-heavy, and look unbalanced; so in a small container, use plants that grow slowly or enjoy limited root runs. Many herbs and alpines, and some of the more compact bedding plants work well in small containers. Choose plants that enjoy the amount of sun or shade they will get in their new positions. This is very important for plants in pots, because a shade-loving plant that likes cool, damp conditions will fry in a sunny place if its roots are confined. In a windy position, make sure the plant is well anchored by the pot.

You can take plants out of beds and try them in the junk pots. This is a particularly good idea in the case of some of the more freely spreading groundcover plants, such as myosotis (forget-me-not), ajuga, or campanula, which can become so invasive in a flowerbed that you may be glad to move them. Many of them look great in junk and, if they have trailing foliage, give the feeling of instant aging. They also integrate well in a bed: plants in a bed mirrored by plants in junk create an attractive rhythm to the scene.

BELOW LEFT **Bedding plants such as primroses bring a splash of color to the garden in the early spring. Mass planted in junk containers, they look simple and confident. Using the same plant in several different containers ties the scene together.**

BELOW CENTER **The circle and the letter "O" dominate the graphic decoration of these milk cartons. The circular yellow flowers of the asteriscus pick up on the strengths of this design.**

BELOW RIGHT **The vertical curved lines that have been etched on the outside of this metal barrel have a strong visual impact. A tree fern not only looks attractive in the planter, but also casts a delicate shadow onto its surface.**

Herbs, alpines, and some bedding plants thrive in small pots.

BELOW Shiny galvanized metal is often planted with simple greens to match the simplicity of the pot. A colorful alternative is to plant nemesia, whose flowers—shown here in shades from white to burnt toffee—appear to bubble out of the bucket.

RIGHT This planting exploits the ornate and complex decoration adorning a fine metal goblet. The simple curved branches of a prostrate rosemary seem to flow out of the swirls on the cup, and the pale blue flowers look soft against the hard metal.

ABOVE, FAR RIGHT When a color is particularly dominant, such as the bright red on this plaid cookie tin, why bother to compete? The geranium looks as if it was born there.

BELOW, FAR RIGHT Bright yellow plastic buckets can be very bright and very yellow. The decision to plant them with yellow calla lilies and place them near other yellow plants makes a virtue out of something that could be a bit too brash for many scenes.

choosing the right plant

When deciding how to plant your junk containers, give preference to plants that fit in with any existing color scheme in the garden, and be wary of introducing too many shades in one area. A garden that tries too hard to incorporate a variety of colors in a small place can be exhausting on the eye, as if the colors are fighting for attention. It is better to focus on a more limited color range. One way to achieve this is to plant a number of junk containers with the same plant in one area.

Try to match the color of flowers or foliage with a color on the junk pot itself—or choose a plant color that uses the pot as a foil. A bright red geranium looks perfectly at home in a can with bright red on it. A powerful primary-colored junk pot often looks best with strong colors, while cool ones look more appropriate with cooler hues such as the silvery gray of bleached wood. The setting makes a difference, however. In a bed full of hot colors, that same bleached container can be planted with hot colors and produce a result that is just as effective. That is why—when it comes to planted junk— guidelines are more appropriate than rules. As your confidence increases, you will come to rely more and more on instinct.

If there is a flower color that you cannot live without (I am partial to apricot), add a splash of paint to the container in a color that coordinates with your favorite. Some pots—especially those in distinctive colors or those made from heavy or rough materials—cry out for strong contrast. In such a case, don't hold back. But don't try to fit too many different colors or shapes into one pot. Multicolored bright flowers of one variety can look powerful, and mass plantings of a single color or a couple of colors can look balanced. A very bright mix of too many colors and flower styles gives an impression of greed and confusion in most garden settings.

Favor plants that keep their looks for more than a couple of weeks. Plenty of bedding varieties have long flowering periods, and there is no shortage of hardy plants that look as attractive in leaf as in flower. (For more information, see the Plant Directory on pages 128–37.)

choosing the right plant

It is advisable to choose plants that harmonize with neighboring plants, and are in keeping with the style of the garden or local area, especially where the neighboring plants are dominated by a particular color, shape, or texture. The more complementary the plants in a group, the more natural the grouping will appear. In a formal garden that includes topiary you could plant your junk with more topiary to maintain the integrity of the garden. Grasses, palms, and bamboos look entirely at home in a tropical-style garden. Alternatively, experiment with a few surprises—which could help open up what might otherwise be a very restrictive style.

Choose plants that are complementary
so the grouping feels natural.

BELOW **The fleshy greenish-gray foliage of an agave stands out powerfully in a modern setting and complements the strong lines of the architecture and the container.**

ABOVE RIGHT **Even though this tree is unlikely ever to produce ripe olives, it looks effective beside the classical ruined column—a juxtaposition that plays on associations with the ancient civilizations of the Mediterranean.**

BELOW RIGHT **A delicate glass lampshade resembles the base of a fountain when the blue lobelia erupts from it. An imaginatively chosen plant can convert the container into something more than it was when unplanted.**

Some of the best junk effects I have seen have involved plants
that together created a coherent story and established a junk
rhythm. Examples of these include a tomato plant in a can that
has a picture of vegetables on it, and shells used as a mulch
on a planted-up plastic bucket. Although such pairings include
an element of gentle surprise, they do not shock.

If the setting has a strong element or theme, you can build
on the illusion. Combining edibles with different types of food
containers feels natural—the lemon-scented thyme in my cake
pan even smells like a delicious cake. A classical column with a
planted fig or olive by it looks as if it could be in ancient Rome
or Athens. In my pond I have planted, in a can, a cordyline
that suggests a purple fountain leaping out of the water.

To me, one of the great advantages of junk planters is that you can move them to create different effects—sometimes grouping them with others, sometimes putting them in a bed or on top of a wall. My tomatoes move around the yard (only three times a year) to be in the sunniest position.

Junk containers have a particular use as temporary homes for plants with short flowering periods. Tulips look gorgeous until after they have flowered, when they soon begin to look ragged. If you keep the tulips in a basic plastic pot and use the junk as an outer sleeve, you can move the tulips into a less visible place after flowering and replace them with planting that promises plenty of summer interest. You can make similar changes to brighten up the yard in the winter, giving prominence to plants such as hellebores that are pretty dull during the rest of the year, or plants such as pansies that are available for planting in the fall.

Junk planters can be rearranged as the seasons change.

RIGHT **Although it will soon outgrow this pot, the viola looks beautiful in its prime.**

ABOVE, CENTER RIGHT **Junk planters as small as these are useful for displaying plants for a short period. A moss rose, which has something artificial about it, goes well with the plastic theme.**

BELOW, CENTER RIGHT **The foliage of a black aeonium is a good match for the dark cauldron.**

FAR RIGHT **A family of teapots has been filled with armeria, which will be planted out when flowering has finished. The teapots can then be refilled to refresh the scene.**

planting

When you discover a junk container, the temptation is to plant it immediately—after all, it may already be pretty old and have survived without much care—but it is often worth spending a bit of time protecting your new treasure against the effects of wet and dry soil, weather conditions, and extremes of temperature.

A good junk pot should last long enough to be enjoyed—even if that is only for a season. Some containers, especially cardboard ones, will be very short-lived and aren't worth protecting. They make a great display for a limited period, and then degrade so badly they can be discarded or even composted.

Wooden containers such as old wine or fruit boxes frequently look more appealing when they have been left untreated—the action of sunlight on wood produces a natural bleached appearance that can be attractive.

Clear preservatives do not stop the bleaching effect, but help inhibit fungal decay. Colored preservatives and specialized horticultural paint (as opposed to water-repellent stain) shields the surface from ultraviolet, preventing bleaching and in some cases compromising the beauty of the wood. A dark preservative will hide the grain of the wood, so test the color on the underside of the container, and leave it to dry, before applying it all over. Don't bother with varnish—unless it is microporous, it tends to bubble when water gets in and does little to prevent decay. Make sure the wood is dry before you apply the preservative both inside and out.

A natural bleached appearance can add to the wood's beauty.

RIGHT, TOP AND CENTER **A new box is coated with colored wood preservative to protect it against decay and the effects of sunlight.**

RIGHT BOTTOM **An older box has been left untreated and allowed to bleach in the sun.**

It will then be necessary to wait at least two weeks before planting the container because most preservatives are poisonous to plants until they are completely dry.

Lining your wooden planter with plastic to the height that the soil will reach and piercing holes in the bottom of the plastic will prevent the salts in the soil from leaching out and staining the surface of the wood. For a box that has widely spaced slats at the base or sides, you can put moss in first to disguise the plastic.

If you are good with tools, you could try burning the surface of the inside of the container with a blowtorch; burned wood does not rot and helps protect the rest of the wood. If your wooden container is held together by metal straps (like many wooden barrels), make sure the straps are

securely attached to the wood. When the wood shrinks in the heat of the day the band can slip down, and the container will fall apart—which is regrettably what happened to my beautiful grape-carrying container. The band should be tacked to the wood in at least three places.

Wicker should always be lined with plastic; if it has a very open weave, insert moss or commercial hanging-basket liner first; it not only looks attractive, but also provides opportunities for planting through the weave.

Cracks in ceramic or stone pots are likely to fracture completely from expansion caused by the freezing of moist soil, but interestingly shaped or textured old pots can look gorgeous secured with a few bands of wire on the outside, which should keep them intact for years. You can hasten the aging of stone and concrete pots, and encourage moss growth, by putting them in the shade and feeding them liquid fertilizer or smearing with fresh horse dung or yogurt.

Metal conducts heat and cold very efficiently and in the heat of the summer can literally fry the roots of your plants, so, after you have made provisions for adequate drainage, line the pot with plastic to protect the roots. With small cans it is often worth putting them in a spot that

BELOW LEFT **Baskets made of wicker and similar natural materials should be lined with plastic to prevent the desirable process of natural decay—which can enhance the appeal of the container—from being speeded up by moisture from the soil.**

BELOW RIGHT **Roughly cut edges at the top of a can are often extremely sharp. To avoid the danger of injuries to the skin it is a good idea to hammer down the edges around the inside of the can. This flattens the edges into a smooth surface.**

OPPOSITE PAGE, ABOVE LEFT **To make drainage holes in a thick plastic container such as this mauve bucket, you need a wood drill and light pressure. Hold the container securely while you are drilling, or you may find that it starts whizzing around with the drill.**

OPPOSITE PAGE, ABOVE RIGHT **Drilling holes in a wooden container such as this wine box is a relatively simple operation. Start drilling at about 1½in (4cm) from one end, and try to space the holes evenly.**

ABOVE **One of the best ways to make drainage holes in a can is to use a hammer and awl, available from hardware stores. Before you start to make the holes, at intervals of 1½in (4cm), place the can on a hard surface such as a solid stone slab or a workbench.**

gets some shade. The cut edge at the top of an old can could be dangerous; before transforming such a can into a junk planter, use a hammer to beat around the inside of the edge and flatten it. Go around with the hammer at least three times, then carefully feel the inside to make sure it is smooth.

Plastic tends to have a limited life because it bleaches and degrades in the sun. There is little point in trying to prevent this, and the bleached look can be preferable anyway.

Most plants require good drainage to thrive. Few junk planters have drainage holes, so these need to be drilled into the bottom of the container—usually at 2½in (6cm) intervals, using a ½in (1cm) wide bit. Drilling into metal is reasonably straightforward, though you can use an awl to pierce drainage holes in old cans. Drilling into stone is a more delicate process. Always use a masonry drill, and support the container on the inside with a block of wood when drilling. Wet the drill as you are drilling to prevent it from getting too hot, and never press down hard. The drill should be allowed to do its job—otherwise, it is easy to crack the whole piece. Drilling anything made of ceramic is very difficult and requires a ceramic drill bit.

Always put broken bits of pot, or shards, into the bottom of the planter to cover the holes, and be generous with them. This stops the soil from falling out of the pot, and prevents the hole from getting blocked up. If your container is more than 12in (30cm) high, put a layer of pebbles on top of the shards. For very delicate pieces, and for most glass, use an inner pot with drainage holes, and put some crushed charcoal at the bottom of the container to keep any water collecting there sweet. Empty the water regularly. You can put marbles both at the bottom of a glass pot and as a mulch over the top. When the water has covered the marbles at the bottom, pour out any excess, covering the pot with your hand to avoid losing any soil.

When planting your container, put in enough soil to make sure the new plant(s) end up about ¾in (2cm) below the top edge. When removing the plant from the pot it has been grown in, gently tease out the roots to encourage new root growth out into the fresh soil. Fill up the pot around the plant(s) and firm in gently. Always water thoroughly just after planting. After a couple of weeks, as the plant settles, the container may need topping off with a little more soil.

Soil-based medium, whose main ingredient is topsoil, holds nutrients and water efficiently, making it a good choice for more permanent plantings, including shrubs and small trees. It is heavy and helps provide stability when the container is placed in a windy situation. Heavy rain or overwatering can increase the weight dramatically, so don't use soil-based medium if load-bearing is an issue, particularly on a balcony.

Soilless medium is usually based on peat or a peat substitute such as coir, bark, or wood fiber. It is light and easy to handle, and, because many plants are bought in peat-based soils, new

FAR LEFT Mulches fulfill a number of purposes. They keep down weeds and help conserve water by limiting evaporation. What's more, they can look great. These shells form a happy association with the plastic bucket, which looks as if it was made to live near the ocean. I've used mussel shells and oyster shells as mulches, but unfortunately have yet to find a similar use for snail shells.

TOP AND CENTER LEFT Mulches can be used to complement the container. The use of tumbled glass chips as a mulch gives this glass container distinction, making the whole display more interesting and slightly less harsh than it otherwise would have been.

BOTTOM LEFT The glass chips also look arresting against the clean lines of a stone container and help to integrate the plant with the pot.

Pebbles, pine cones, shells, and other mulches add a stylish finishing touch to junk planting.

plants start well in them. They are suitable for annuals and other less permanent plantings, and where load-bearing may be a concern. The main problem with soilless mediums is that they need more regular watering and feeding than soil-based ones, and must never be permitted to dry out completely because it is very difficult to remoisten them. There is now a mixture available that contains imidacloprid, which combats aphids and vine weevils.

Ericaceous mixture should be used in containers for plants that require an acid soil, such as camellias and rhododendrons. Water-retaining granules can be a valuable addition to the mixture, particularly when you are planting a thirsty plant like bamboo, but don't be tempted to add too many—or the plant will end up sitting in a spongy mess unable to absorb nutrients.

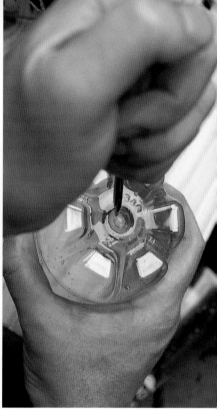

Decorative mulches have several advantages. They help prevent weeds and reduce the amount of watering required, as well as adding to the attractiveness of your junk pot. Old pieces of shell, bits of pine cone, pebbles, and similar items can be matched to the plant in the container— pine cones under a pine look wonderful, for example. Add mulch only when the soil is already moist.

The smaller the planter the more quickly it will dry out, particularly if it is made of a porous material such as terracotta or wood. A sunny and windy position increases transpiration and evaporation dramatically. You need to know the specific requirements of your plants—which vary widely—but it is generally helpful to use saucers or trays under your pots to keep a small reservoir of water. In the height of summer most pots need to be watered twice a day. Be generous: continue watering until the soil is soaking and water is draining through the holes. An automatic watering system, available at garden centers, can be valuable, especially when you are on vacation.

The shape of your junk container makes a substantial difference to the amount of watering it needs; for example, a wide shallow planter dries out more quickly than a deep one would. Containers with narrow tops and wider middles lose less water through surface evaporation, but watering them can be tricky. In the case of a larger container, sink the lower half of a plastic bottle with tiny holes punched in its base into the compost, with the top slightly protruding from the top of the container. This can be used as a water reservoir and will help keep the soil moist longer.

If you are going on vacation and no one is available to water your pots, move as many of them as you can into the shade. An extra precaution against drying out is to sink terracotta and other porous containers slightly into soil. In containers that have dried out completely, the soil often shrinks away from the sides, and any water simply runs down the insides, missing the soil. If this happens to one of your pots, put it in a bucket of water until the soil is waterlogged and heavy.

OPPOSITE PAGE **To keep your planter well watered right to the lower roots, create a reservoir by sinking into the soil the lower half of a plastic bottle with tiny holes pierced in the base. Traditional methods of watering often concentrate the water near the surface and down the sides of the pot, which is where the roots would develop. This little reservoir helps take the water to the center of the pot, encouraging the roots to use all the soil in the container. It also means that, when you water your plant, it receives a thorough watering rather than a mere sprinkling.**

Sink a dry container into a bucket of water and leave it there until it is waterlogged and heavy.

Reduce watering as the growing season ends, and check in winter that the containers have not dried out completely. Some plants, including bamboos and evergreen shrubs, continue to transpire in winter, and need to be checked at least once a week in dry weather, particularly during mild winters. Plants in containers also require regular feeding. Peat-based medium needs more frequent feeding than soil-based mixtures, and frequent watering leaches away the nutrients.

The easiest method of feeding is to use slow-release granules, which can last up to six months after an application. Liquid feeds provide a more immediate pick-me-up and need to be applied every two weeks during the growing season. For flowering and fruiting plants, use a high-potash preparation, such as tomato food, just before and during flowering. For plants that are grown for their foliage, use high-nitrogen fertilizer. Do not overfeed, particularly if you are using a powder, which can scorch the leaves and burn the roots. Always water the plants after applying solid fertilizers.

In the fall, for permanent planting, you can scrape off the first ¾in (2cm) of soil and topdress with composted manure or fresh compost—but this is no substitute for regular feeding during the growing season.

Removing dead flowers from geraniums, petunias, pansies, and other bedding plants prolongs the flowering period and prevents the display from looking tired. Cut off the flowers at the first leaf bud with shears or nip them with your fingernails. Tiny flowers such as alyssum, lobelia, and impatiens continue to flower without deadheading. Deadhead perennials if the old flower heads are unsightly.

A plant that has become potbound—or outgrown its container—needs to be repotted. For advice on how to repot, see the instructions outlined below and the photographs on the opposite page.

One problem sometimes encountered with junk planters is that their irregular shapes can make repotting difficult. For example, a planted can with a narrow opening at the top and a wider body has to be hacksawed if repotting becomes necessary. For this reason, I tend to choose either annuals or plants that can last for many seasons without repotting for these types of container.

ABOVE **If you are faced with the prospect of repotting a plant, the task will be much easier if the original container you chose has a shape as simple as this rectangular wood box. The new container into which you move your plant should be at least 2in (5cm) wider than the original one; for a big plant, it should be at least 4in (10cm) wider.**

When your plants
need to be transferred
into a larger container,
seize the opportunity
to experiment with junk.

OPPOSITE PAGE **If you need to repot a plant that has outgrown its container, start by removing the plant from its original pot when it is dry and the rootball has shrunk away from the sides of the pot. Then gently tease out the roots from the solid rootball and put the plant into a larger junk container with fresh potting mixture. Drench the repotted plant with water. Then drench again.**

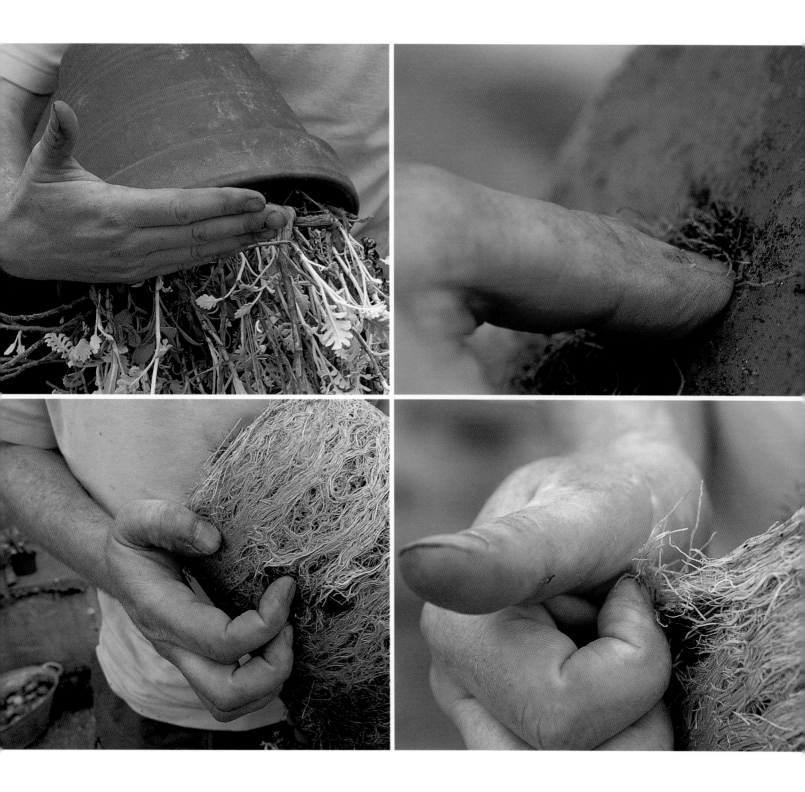

Delicate pots that need to be kept frostfree should be moved inside in the winter. The best plants for these are summer annuals, or conservatory plants such as citrus fruits that themselves need winter protection. Some pots can simply be emptied of soil, turned upside down and stored outside. This prevents expansion of the soil in the container as a result of frost. To avoid waterlogged soil it is worth removing the saucers (if you have them) from underneath your pots in the fall.

To allow your junk plantings to thrive you need to devise a strategy to see off slugs and snails.

ABOVE **Deadheading certain plants pays dividends. This pink geranium has continued to flower longer than it would have otherwise because the old flowers have been removed as soon as they were past their best. Deadheading also makes a plant look fresher and more attractive.**

Slugs and snails seem able to scale any height to satisfy their insatiable appetites. Smearing petroleum jelly just below the rim of the container can be an effective deterrent. Keep an eye out for the little beasts in shady, dank places where pots are grouped together. Once you know where they congregate, check the area regularly in the evening with a flashlight. I use my delicious hosta—it seems to be the plant most tempting to slugs and snails early in the season—as a lure, so I know where to hunt for best results. There are also beer traps and slug pellets, but choose those that do not harm other wildlife. I have found that a coarse sand mulch around vulnerable plants such as hostas can help a little. Don't throw the snails into a neighbor's yard unless you want to start a snail war.

Vine weevils can also be a menace. The weevil larvae (wrinkled white curled-up grubs) eat roots, and the first sign of an attack may be the complete collapse of the plant. The beetle is slow-moving and eats out notches in the leaves of shrubs, particularly euonymuses and rhododendrons. You can now buy nematodes that act as a biological control and should help contain numbers. Remove isolated weevils; if there is a serious infestation, remove the plant and soil, put them in a plastic bag, seal and throw it away.

LEFT Slugs are not particularly attractive and can be a serious nuisance in a garden. Junk pots provide some appealingly shady and dank habitats, so when you go slug hunting in the evening, expect to find a few slimy trails. Smearing the rim of a container with petroleum jelly forms a good barrier.

ABOVE This snail must have been trained in camouflage skills. It was trying to infiltrate a pot by disguising itself as one of the shells being collected for a mulch—but it was betrayed by its color and the fact that it was seen moving slowly.

Junk containers come in a huge range of styles, materials,
shapes, and colors, which makes them difficult to classify.
Here they are arranged according to material: ceramics, stone and glass;
wood and wicker; metal; and plastic and rubber; the last section shows
some of the effects you can achieve by mixing materials.
One of the most charming aspects of gardening with planted junk
is the slightly eccentric forms of container that you are bound to find.

PART TWO

planted junk

ceramics, stone, and glass

Many ceramic objects that you will come across were deliberately designed to be shown off.

Ceramics offer a wonderful choice of designs and colors, and pieces with planting potential can be picked up cheaply in a variety of junk-hunting paradises.

The starting point for many of the most accessible ceramic junk containers is the kitchen. From cups and mugs to large bowls, this is an area of rich pickings. Small receptacles can be used to hold plants temporarily, thought often cups are too small and, being narrow at the base, tend to be top-heavy and

OPPOSITE PAGE **A stylish ceramic kettle sits snugly in a narrow bed. In common with many other food-related containers that are moved into the garden, it looks as much at home here as it would in a kitchen.**

BELOW LEFT **A stone and shell ornament with a distinctive homemade quality brightens up an area under a tree. Shells, even when stuck onto a pot in this way, fit naturally into many styles of garden.**

BELOW **These white kitchen molds—which were originally intended for making gelatin desserts—are a beautiful addition to the garden. They carry echoes of an earlier historical era, and you almost expect to see a figure in pilgrim dress emerging from the background prepared to start cooking a great feast. Such containers deserve to be planted with something that does nothing to obscure the beauty of their shape.**

ceramics, stone, and glass

unstable when planted. Mugs are a safer bet—and, because the choice of designs is so numerous, they give plenty of scope to have fun. Their association with coffee breaks and taking it easy also makes them relaxed junk planters to have around, but their smallness means that they fill up with water quickly and need to be emptied after rain.

Ceramic vases make excellent junk containers in that they were created to enhance and be enhanced by floral and foliage displays. They are straightforward to plant and often look best when used to display plants at their most attractive. The intricate designs of many ceramic pieces provide plenty of imaginative opportunities, and it is often possible to highlight a particular color within the pattern by choosing a flower color or leaf shade that matches it.

A well-chosen junk container can look so natural amid the garden greenery that the memory of its original use is a nostalgic recollection.

ceramics, stone, and glass

FAR LEFT **This shallow and delicate ceramic bowl appears to be under the protection of a couple of guardians. The subtle colors and suggestion of fruit give it a gentle feel. The saxifrage flowers reach up delicately and do not overwhelm the container.**

CENTER LEFT **Although made of terracotta, these pots were not originally meant for outdoor use; on the contrary, they may have been molds used in a factory. The buildup of residue on the outside gives them a well-worn feel that is mirrored by the use of a cristata fern, which conveys the same sense of antiquity. The finely divided leaves of the fern seem to reflect the heavily marked surface of the molds.**

LEFT **The same delicate ceramic bowl has been moved to a place where it appears to be part of the planting. The baby's tears that covers the ground makes a lovely cushion to place the bowl on.**

It seems that the modern world of plastic bottles and cartons has made most ceramic pitchers redundant except as ornaments. Take advantage of this, and give them a new job in the garden. The beautiful designs were made to be shown off, and having foliage and flowers in and around them can make them look as if they were born to be plant containers.

This can be one of the peculiarities of a well-chosen junk planter: it looks so natural amid the greenery that knowledge of its original use is no barrier to its horticultural renaissance. Ceramics chip and crack easily, which means that the junk hunter can find some wonderful bargains. The chips and cracks may require a bit of wiring up, and even protection from the frost in winter, but the pot looks all the better in the garden because it has lived a little.

ceramics, stone, and glass

ABOVE, FAR LEFT **Concrete blocks from a builders' yard are easy to convert into junk pots. The holes are a good size for many plants, especially bedding ones such as these double-flowered impatiens.**

ABOVE, LEFT AND RIGHT **A cracked ceramic sink with the perfect drainage hole has become a generous-sized planter. The tropical grass seems to reach out in an almost surreal way, and the mulch of** white stone chips blends sympathetically with the clinical edges of the sink.

BELOW LEFT **Chunky structures such as concrete blocks can be useful for establishing boundaries in a yard. Here they have been placed at right angles to each other to give clearer definition to a corner.**

BELOW RIGHT **This cinderblock has a contemporary feel, and looks particularly appropriate** in a modern setting. It has been transformed into a container after being hollowed out with a hammer and chisel. (If you decide to attempt this yourself, don't get impatient; gentle taps are needed to remove little chunks.) The curved striations are original and seems to flow from the ground up. The succulent-looking hens-and-chicks are ideal partners for this style of container and need a minimum of soil to thrive.

An object as heavy and solid as a stone trough can be planted to create a surprisingly delicate effect.

Stone troughs are harder to locate and are staggeringly heavy—but if you can find one it will make an extraordinary addition to your garden. Such containers are so solid and permanent that they seem to have an immovable obstinacy about them, as if they were not simply prehistoric, but able to outlast everything else. Troughs planted with slow-growing alpines can become miniature gardens in themselves. Ironically for something so solid, the effect of a trough can be very delicate. The stone should be kept pretty bare so as not to conceal its beauty.

Although less attractive, concrete troughs can serve a valuable purpose—and should be planted in such a way as to hide some of the hard surface. Sinks and bathtubs have pre-drilled drainage holes, and make great horticultural containers because of the volume of soil they can hold—but any bathtub would have to be exceptionally attractive to make it into my yard. I have seen one used to good effect in a vegetable patch.

ABOVE **This unplanted chimney pot throws a honeysuckle into dramatic relief. Such a pairing demonstrates the effectiveness in a display of concealing part of a junk planter in such a way that it appears to be planted even when it is not.**

RIGHT **There are some gems that can speak for themselves without the need for much planting. We found these terracotta wine storage sleeves in a basement. Placed on the gorgeous York stone and planted with bronze fennel, they create an effect that is simple and exquisite.**

A plant in a chimney pot can give an illusion of a drift of smoke.

RIGHT **When Heath Robinson died, my dad took over—as this construction shows. A solid chimney pot can prove to be an excellent planter, although it requires plenty of feed. Dad made the frame from home-grown black bamboo, which can be seen in the background.**

BELOW **The clematis has been deeply planted in the chimney pot to keep its roots cool and in the shade. The height of the pot helps to display the early spring show of shoots—a sight that is often missed when the plant is viewed at ground level. This example shows how to use a deep junk planter to provide favorable horticultural conditions for a hungry plant.**

Among the most commonly used junk planters are chimney pots. Their depth and relative narrowness make them unusual as containers, and the material from which they are made (baked clay or terracotta) is one that is familiar to gardeners, which makes the transition into the garden appear natural. I prefer very plain ones, and like to see a simple planting that relies on a limited color scheme. The silvery leaf of a plant such as a helichrysum looks like a drift of smoke, which can create a magical effect. Chimney pots also add height to a flowerbed and offer fantastic drainage and stability.

There are some junk planters that are made of similar materials, including quite rare clay molds, and various types of jars, from Ali Baba to Cretan, which are often sold as garden ornaments and can look good near water or planted with something that creates a fountain of leaves, such as a cordyline.

If the shape and esthetics alone were to determine the number of junk planters available, then glass would have a chapter all to itself. Glasses, bottles, glass bowls, and pitchers often have beautiful shapes; they look particularly elegant when full of plants—wine bottles, for example, make fine vases—and can fit very comfortably into a garden. But glass is fragile and breaks easily. It is also difficult to make drainage holes in it, so leave this task to a glass-drilling expert; and cutting the necks off bottles leaves some sharp edges that could be dangerous. There are some glass objects that already have holes in their bases, such as lampshades, but they are seldom transparent, which is a shame.

Some sleek glass containers have their places in restrained minimalist gardens, and in gardens with strong architectural links to houses with a lot of glass in their construction. This exemplifies how junk planters can be used sympathetically in the garden to mirror materials used in the house.

BELOW, FAR LEFT AND CENTER LEFT Glass can give a container a new dimension—and watching the development of the root system can be quite fascinating. Roots always grow away from light, so keep the glass partly in shade.

ABOVE LEFT Using a glass as a temporary pot for a flowering plant can quickly and quietly fill a gap. The fluting on the glass fits in well with the backgound, and the colour of the impatiens helps form a pink foundation for the rest of the view.

LEFT Glass is a happy addition to a modern garden, especially near water. These two glasses filled with *Carex* 'Frosted Curls' (an ornamental grass) have been placed in such a way as to reinforce the existing symmetry.

ABOVE Glass marbles used as a mulch and for drainage at the bottom create balance in a pot.

Particularly valuable to the junk gardening enthusiast are ceramic teapots and coffeepots, which can be amusing and genteel in a garden. Small branches and shoots flowing out of the top of the pot, with flowers trickling down the sides, can produce a poetic effect. Transplanting plants out of such pots can be virtually impossible, so confine your choice to annuals, alpines, and herbs. Search your own closets before looking elsewhere; many of us have spare tea and coffeepots that haven't tasted caffeine for years.

The same advice can be given in respect of many of the bowls and jars used to store and display foodstuffs. Try to find the ones that have lost their lids, of which there are plenty, as they can no longer serve any useful purpose in the kitchen. I tend to keep the attractive complete ones for storing my tea, sugar, and coffee—but as soon as the lid of a piece has been broken it finds itself storing a plant instead, and overflowing with flowers.

BELOW LEFT **When I found this lidless crocodile teapot, I had to give him groovy hair. The creeping thyme makes him look creative—and very cool.**

RIGHT **Although this chicken looks slightly surprised to have become a planter, the orange tones of the lantana flowers pick up on the splashes of orange on the bird's neck and head. Try to highlight the beauty of a piece by using complementary colors.**

Quirky ceramics bring color and humor to dark corners.

Some designs, particularly those shaped like animals, can give the impression that they have walked, hopped, or flown into your yard—and found an ideal place to make their home.

There are some bizarre bits and pieces that may appeal to the real junkaholic. One of the first ceramic junk planters I saw was a urinal on an outside wall, filled with strawberries. The runners overflowing it created a disturbingly familiar vision—and even though the juicy red fruits looked good enough to eat, I just couldn't motivate myself to pick them. Such items may be amusing additions to a garden, but use them with care. They will conjure up images that are usually irrelevant to a garden. They only natural place for a urinal would be near the compost heap, particularly as the occasional late-night wander into the yard could be a great compost accelerator.

wood and wicker

The most natural material for junk planters is wood. It came from the soil, and it fits in beautifully when it returns to its place of birth. In between it may have done any of a wide variety of jobs—from aging and flavoring alcohol to providing the people of Holland with durable footwear. Heavy-duty wood is an excellent material for planters because it provides such good insulation from the extremes of heat and cold.

Boxes made of soft wood are still used for the packaging and transporting of some premium labels of wine. These wine boxes are easy to obtain, and are one of my favorite additions to a garden. They introduce a peculiar touch of class: a box printed with the name of a claret lifts the whole tone of the garden. The most appropriate plant for a wine box would be a grapevine, but these grow more successfully either in deep containers or in the ground, so better alternatives would be edibles or flowers that allow the beauty of the wine box to show through. There are small single-bottle boxes that are rarer

Wooden junk containers look **entirely natural** when they are planted and reintroduced to the soil—the place where they were born.

OPPOSITE PAGE, LEFT Wine boxes can look as appealing in the garden, overflowing with plants, as they do when full of bottles of wine. I can almost smell the fine bouquet as these gorgeous red and rosé primroses spill out of the top.

OPPOSITE PAGE, RIGHT Wood is a natural partner for many plants. When teamed with a floriferous mature *Helleborus niger*, this box makes a sensational sight in winter. The neutral color of the wood means that the flowers are the star of the show. The container can be moved into the shade in summer.

LEFT AND ABOVE LEFT You have to let your imagination roam freely to work out the origins of some finds. The strength of these highly unusual wooden boxes lies in their shape, and the number 7 brings touch of mystery to the scene: the question "seven whats?" is left hanging in the air. Salmon-pink geraniums make a satisfying combination with the cool gray wood.

ABOVE Old painted wood—particularly if it is slightly decayed where the grain is clearly visible, as in this old carrying box—is a real piece of junk treasure. When you have a container with such an attractive surface, find plants that complement its color and texture. Simply filling the box with sage gives it just the right look and feeling.

Weathered wooden boxes bring a feeling of deep calm and serenity.

to find and can be mass planted with a single type of plant. If you manage to acquire such a lovely junk planter, keep some of it visible rather than overwhelming it with trailing plants, which will not only hide the wood but also encourage rotting and stop the sun bleaching it.

Older wooden boxes, often made of a hard wood, can help create a wonderful feeling of serenity in a garden; for me, the slightly decayed and silvered look of some old boxes conjures up thoughts of the sea. Like beautiful driftwood on a beach, an old wooden box well placed in a garden seems to have arrived at its resting place. There are some great

sources for these boxes, and weathered planks and pieces of wood can frequently be found in secondhand stores in seaside towns. Planks can be useful as the basis for homemade junk planters or as edging for a bed.

There are plenty of other wooden boxes that have potential as junk planters, from little ornamental storage boxes to old-fashioned tea chests. But beware of the weight of larger boxes: a tea chest full of soil may be in danger of bursting, particularly after heavy rain; put something light and bulky, such as broken styrofoam trays, at the bottom, and wait at least a week after filling the chest with soil before you plant, to allow the soil to settle. Tea chests, because they are so big, offer many opportunities for junk planting; for example, fast-growing annual edibles such as corn or tomatoes grow well and look perfectly at home in them. Leave large

OPPOSITE PAGE, LEFT **A rack of pigeonhole shelves from an office has been planted in a crisscross pattern to highlight its strengths.**

OPPOSITE PAGE, RIGHT **An old wooden drawer makes a simple and shallow junk planter that is nevertheless deep enough for bedding plants such as alyssum.**

BELOW LEFT **Old wooden filing cabinet drawers are often ornate and impressive. The delicate pale green foliage of an epimedium looks particularly attractive against the mellow background.**

BELOW **This partitioned shelf, once used in a grocery store, fits onto the ledge and blends with the warm colors of the coleus leaves.**

boxes empty long enough to be sure that you have made the right decision about where to place them—because you certainly don't want to have to move them after they have been planted.

Smaller boxes and wooden drawers that may have originated in offices can be transformed into lovely showcases for displaying small plants. More unusual are pigeonhole shelves with numerous partitions, which look effective when selectively planted. If you come across such an interesting object, consider how to highlight its strengths. Planting every compartment would quickly disguise its look, so leave some empty to create a pattern between the plants. Wooden drawers from ancient filing cabinets have less of an "office administration" feel than modern metal drawers.

Barrels are often sold as planters, so I prefer to mention here some of the less common ones, particularly agricultural examples, such as an old butter churn—a beautiful and evocative object in itself that may look best in a garden left unplanted and treated simply as an ornament.

BELOW LEFT **Bamboo is as natural a material as you could wish to find for a junk container. This bamboo planter is big enough for a few shallow-rooting plants, which should be kept moist in the shade. A dwarf bamboo such as the *Pleioblastus auricomus* would be great for a season.**

BELOW CENTER **Some planted junk is weird and wonderful. This dried pod has probably come from Africa or Asia and looks like a boat carrying a cargo of other unusual ornaments.**

BELOW RIGHT **There are often little patches of a garden that are neither grass nor bed but, depending on the weather, closely resemble either baked earth or mud. A beautiful wood bowl covers such a patch and is integral to a corner planting. The mellow color merges well with the hostas, and dwarf grasses reflect the straplike leaves of the cordyline above.**

ABOVE **Old barrels can often be bought from garden centers, but I particularly like the really junky ones that look as if they have had interesting lives. The sturdiness of an old barrel** means that it is a useful basis for a pavement planting.

ABOVE RIGHT **The well-worn look of this lacquered papier-mâché bowl makes it an apt** item in a garden, where nature encourages imperfections; a fuchsia adds to the harmony.

BELOW, LEFT AND RIGHT **A nut shell and a curvaceous bowl** of unknown origin suggest a tropical garden. They have been planted with a cycad to create a beautiful balance between pot and contents.

Emphasize your pot's strengths.

Wooden bowls are also prey to the junk hunter—for example, an old salad bowl planted with cut-and-come-again lettuce is a treat. Coconut half-shells can be great as temporary plant holders, particularly in a party setting, when they can convey a "piña colada" feel. Other bowls worth looking out for include those of African or other ethnic design, which fit well into a garden filled with tropical plants.

Wooden crates used for transporting fruit and vegetables are almost always desperately thin because they are made to be thrown away as soon as the retailer has finished with them— but they make a lovely temporary addition to a garden and are particularly appropriate to stand pots of plants in. Such crates may have colorful designs on paper stapled to them—as these are often pictures of fresh produce, they can make a garden look very productive. Both the thin wood and the paper will rot quickly, and lifting a crate full of plants once it has been in the garden for a couple of months is almost too simple— because the base, and the plants, are usually left behind. Older food crates were made to last and are far more substantial, but they are also far more difficult to find.

The most temporary of junk containers are those made of cardboard. They are worth using only if they are really special —my Glenfiddich whisky container has lasted well through a typical English summer of rain and showers. There are also some fine designs on boxes, particularly those once used for fruit and vegetables, which can easily benefit the garden before they rot away. Some of the colors and images on them are really lively, and if you can match the plant with the picture, it may appear that your garden is about to start supplying the local market. But cardboard is no more than compressed paper and will disintegrate quickly, perhaps leaving a mushy "footprint" that appears to be a safe haven for woodlice.

Waxed paper, commonly found in drinks cartons, is made of stronger stuff that is meant to be waterproof, but it still rots quickly. Cartons are best reserved for young plants and edibles, and again are often adorned with lovely images. Milk cartons, which have agricultural connotations, fit happily into an

ABOVE **It is surprising how attractive packaging can be. For example, a cardboard box with tiny checks is a gem as a short-term junk planter. Placed near a wall, where it has some shelter from the rain, it will last longer than it would in an exposed position (though still not for long). The flowers of phygelius look playful and delicate.**

RIGHT **Cardboard fruit and vegetable boxes come from all over the world, and the colors, patterns, and words printed on them can transport you to another continent. Even if they last for only a few weeks, such boxes bring pleasure.**

ABOVE, FAR RIGHT **Black and yellow in a garden—and it's not a wasp. Even the name, Cleopatra, is evocative, and the container cannot fail to be beautiful. It makes a rather splendid temporary home for these cosmos.**

BELOW, FAR RIGHT **A strange garlic box—whose maker was carried away by the power of marketing—is having a short stay in the garden; it is filled with mimulus (monkey flower), which match the dominant color.**

Cardboard adds notes of vibrancy and bright colors.

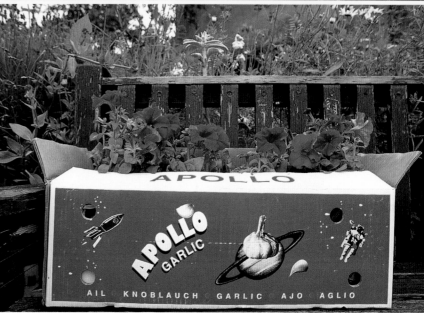

ABOVE, FAR LEFT **A seasonal display of begonias in a small wicker basket looks natural on a patio, particularly because the scale of the plant is in keeping with the shallow container.**

ABOVE LEFT **Wicker shopping bags make attractive and versatile temporary planters. This yellow day lily remains in a plastic container and will be planted out in the garden when it has finished flowering.**

BELOW, FAR LEFT **A lovely balance is achieved by using the width and flexibility of this simple basket to mirror the fantail of the blue hesper palm.**

BELOW LEFT **An intricately woven wicker bag filled with delicate flowers and surrounded by bold architectural foliage sits comfortably in a bed.**

Wicker baskets are quite at home filled with flowers, and they blend subtly into the background or foreground of a garden.

eclectic country scene, and mango juice cartons can help to strengthen a tropical setting. These are examples of how junk containers can be used as elements in a larger scheme that is designed to create an illusion.

Wicker baskets are rarely ostentatious and, being well behaved in polite beds, they look graceful and perfectly at home filled with flowers; they integrate well as a background or foreground for other plants.

In addition to being exceptionally versatile, wicker is made from dried and woven plant stems, so it fits naturally into most garden settings. Whether in a cottage garden where pastel shades dominate or a tropical bed with palms and grasses, the browns and grays of wicker merge with the tones of other plants easily and sympathetically. More unusual wicker items, such as old-fashioned laundry baskets, are slightly more provocative.

ABOVE LEFT **Delicate foliage set against the architectural shapes of a lantern-shaped wicker basket highlights the strengths of the container and the natural beauty of the material. It would seem wasteful to swamp it with leaves and flowers.**

ABOVE RIGHT **When set against such a bold background, this simple basket requires the flower power of daisies to show it off to best advantage.**

Wicker shopping baskets are more flamboyant still and can produce an entertaining effect in a more eclectic garden—but they are unlikely to survive long because they are vulnerable to rotting at the base.

Using discarded bits of furniture such as simple wooden chairs, which are easy to convert into containers, can be effective, especially if you use plants that grow to form a "cushion"; these include many alpines, and herbs such as camomile—which is lovely to sit on and has historically been used for this purpose. Chairs look at ease near a house wall, where you would be likely to see other outdoor furniture. Old pieces of furniture are easy to find—in dumpsters, for example—or can be bought cheaply.

A number of wooden containers with junk-planting possibilities once had industrial functions, for example giant cable holders, but many items of this sort are too big for the standard-sized garden and very awkward to

ABOVE LEFT **The decaying state of this painted and planted wooden chair adds to the charm of the scene, and the saxifrage and sedum help hold it together. Reserve shallow junk containers for shallow-rooting plants such as some of the alpines.**

BELOW LEFT **The chair gives the garden a restful feel, but it would not be very comfortable to sit on its sedum cushion. Our canine friend has obviously worked this out already.**

ABOVE **A former industrial cable holder is now used as a table, with a hole in its center for a display. Treat such a container as you would a vase of flowers, by simply inserting in the hole a vibrant-looking potted plant like this linum.**

ABOVE RIGHT **For me, the cable holder evokes memories of a book called *The fields beneath: how nature will come back after we've neglected it*.**

Tables, chairs, and other pieces of old furniture can be transformed into the most original junk planters of all.

carry through the house. I had a gardening friend who once found a cable holder, but ended up having to scrap it because he was unable to get it through the doorway of his house and out into the yard. This may appear an entirely predictable outcome, but it is all too easy to find yourself in such a position when enthusiasm and creativity conspire to strangle practicality and common sense.

Modern packaging often involves wooden items. My brother recently spotted some discarded wooden casings used to protect computers in transit. We marched these home, to rather curious looks from passers-by, but their length and obvious sturdiness augurs well for their future in my garden.

Old toys are powerfully
evocative of another era.

Wooden toy trucks and trailers are joyous additions to a garden, and can make good planters for colorful bedding or billowing perennial plants. This is another opportunity to choose plants that complement the container: a toy is a playful object, so fill it with plants that are fun. Even though they are miniatures, they give the impression of being on the move, taking a cargo from the house to the garden or between flowerbeds. They are also powerfully evocative of another era, both in history and as a reminder of what being young used to be like before TV and computers. But bear in mind that young kids still love them and may make straight for them, regardless of the fragility and delicacy of nearby plantings. Unfortunately, such toys are no longer as inexpensive as they were, although garage sales are a good source. Other wooden toys that make interesting plant containers are wooden boats, which look great near a pond. I would be tempted to line delicate objects such as these with plastic and stand pots in them instead of fully planting them.

I find wooden clogs more confusing as shoes than as planters. Their Dutch connections make them entirely appropriate in a garden, but it does not follow that you are obliged to plant them with tulips. Some shoes look quite silly as planters—I saw a pair of sawn-off hip boots full of petunias looking like an unsightly pair of sawn-off boots—but Dutch clogs do add something to the right flowerbed.

ABOVE, FAR LEFT **These old toy boats—set against a weathered blue wall, on a plank suspended over gravel—reinforce the impression of being near the sea under a watery sky. As demonstrated here, even the smallest details can have a fundamental effect on the atmosphere of a garden.**

ABOVE LEFT **After the initial surprise of seeing a pair of clogs sticking out from beneath a plant, it becomes** clear that they fit well into the garden scene. The purple ajuga looks comfortable in its new junk home.

BELOW, FAR LEFT **Built as a garden ornament, a run-down wooden windmill makes an appropriate transition to a junk planter. Windmills evoke associations with another era and the flat landscapes of The Netherlands. The proximity of the red tulips reinforces the Dutch connections.**

BELOW, CENTER LEFT **Toy trucks could have been built to be mobile junk planters, but they are quite difficult to find. The link with travel conveys the sense that these nemesia are on their way to a new destination.**

LEFT **Picking up on the warm umber tones of the clogs, these burnt-orange marigolds seem to melt into the wood of the clogs, whose gentle patterns look like an abstract reflection of the flower.**

For real junkoholics—those people who are determined to have the ultimate in junk gardens—wood offers some wonderful opportunities to indulge in fantasy. The delights on offer range from bits of found art, such as hollowed-out tree trunks, to, if you are really lucky, remnants of wooden boats. Items of found wooden junk can resemble beautiful sculptures that require little planting to look their best. Pieces of driftwood can be used simply as garden ornaments or tied together to create a holder for a pot.

I have discovered that dumpsters are a bountiful source of the bits of wood that I tack together to make my rather slapdash wooden outer garments for pots; particularly useful items include old railroad ties and roof beams. I once saw a

Some items of found art resemble beautiful sculptures.

coffin being used as a giant planter. Even though it was reasonably weatherproof, strong, and a marvelously generous size for plants, it was one of the most inappropriate and spooky garden additions I have ever seen; the discomfort it produced in me greatly amused its owner.

A quirky object such as an old wood and leather collar that once formed part of a plow harness can make a splendid surround to a mass planting when simply placed in a bed—and could be particularly appealing to people with an interest in horses. Other leather-covered items such as old suitcases can create beautiful settings for plants and bring a real vacation feeling into a garden. These objects will have to be sacrificed to their fate at the hands of the elements, so only cases that have passed their travel-by date should be used for this purpose.

OPPOSITE PAGE, ABOVE AND BELOW
After the great storms in Britain in 1987 there was a multitude of damaged and blown-down trees. Hollowing out part of a tree trunk with a chisel to make a junk planter was one way to take advantage of the disaster.

ABOVE Trunks can also be pieces of found art, nature's sculptures. Take the opportunity to convert a piece of nature's debris into a useful garden object.

RIGHT AND FAR RIGHT A horse's collar of wood and leather has been put in a border to encircle a clump of snow-in-summer, whose flowers harmonize beautifully with the weathered paint. Junk planters do not always have to be converted into containers; they can simply be incorporated into existing plantings as they were found.

Allumettes

metal

Metallic storage vessels and containers can survive for years, creating an enormous choice of junk planters. Unlike cardboard cartons, cans cannot be easily crushed, nor do they collapse the way thin naked wooden boxes do. If they were originally made to contain food or liquid, cans also have a natural reservoir for soil.

Metal junk lasts well when placed outside, even improving with age. A little bit of rust, gradually spreading into a soft russeting, fits wonderfully in a garden. Corrosion is part of the natural process of growing old, and in a world of pretend perfection it is comforting to see the elements at work. After all, plants are not perfect; they have blemishes on leaves, unbalanced growth, and marks on stems. Signs of aging are one of the most attractive aspects of many junk containers—which is why I get impatient to see them on new terracotta, wood and stone.

Stainless steel does not weather well, however, and is more difficult to use in the garden. "Stainless" does not mean "scratchless" or "smearless", and the blemishes that occur on the mirrored surface can be irritating rather than attractive. On the other hand, galvanized metal, which has been coated with rust-resistant zinc, looks comfortable in many garden settings. It lacks the sheen of stainless steel and is not prone to decay in the same way as untreated metals.

Once you have opened your mind to using metal containers as planters, the opportunities may seem to swamp you. So don't hurry. Take your time and if you find something really good, go for it. Some objects will be brand new. Some will be quite old and appear to be unwanted; an old vase you have grown tired of or a baking pan that became unemployed the moment

FAR LEFT **Tin cans newly planted with ferns, grasses, and a dwarf hebe fit well into a garden because they once held agricultural produce.**

LEFT **A weathered container retains its vitality and interest,** and the bare metal framed by the disappearing label gives an arty impression.

ABOVE RIGHT **The cans in my garden have been chosen to harmonize with the wider scene, which is pretty eclectic.**

Signs of aging are among the most attractive aspects
of many junk containers. In a world of pretend perfection,
it is comforting to see the elements at work.

LEFT AND FAR LEFT **Some cans are so stylish that they could have been designed as cutting-edge containers. Considering that my local delicatessen was delighted to give me these, I rate them as great value. When filling such wonderful junk pots, try to be consistent in the planting. The simple repetition of the box balls helps to highlight their beauty.**

RIGHT **Drinks cans with bright labels are fun for small plants such as this dark pansy. I favor the San Pellegrino label because it is evocative of my early family vacations in Italy. You can use junk to bring some of your own nostalgia into a garden.**

BELOW **Old metal cans with lids can add to the character of a garden. Primroses have an old-fashioned feel that makes them appropriate partners for this particular container.**

Olive cans from France and Greece seem to grow in my garden, mingling with cans that held pickles or tomatoes.

the supermarkets wafted the smell of baking bread into the air can be given a new job in the garden. The smallest metal containers likely to be of use are some of the food cans; even tiny ones can be used for growing seedlings. In a natural or wild garden, leaving a paper label on a can adds an extra element of interest because, when the label rots, it exposes the surface of the can and contributes to the "lived-in" look.

Used well, a can or group of cans can look stylish in a garden, and appear to best advantage when placed on a hard surface such as a corner of a patio or the top of a low wall. Somehow the hard surfaces of the garden marry well with the metal. Cans can also be treated to make their appearance more interesting—simply adding a coat of paint is a good way to

Gloss paint weathers and peels.

do this. Painted cans can be a valuable addition to a garden, particularly when the summer bedding is ready for planting. Some of the paint colors can bring a new dimension to the character of your garden. You can use either standard gloss paint—which weathers and peels rather nicely—or more specialized metal paint, including car paint.

Drinks cans, which are usually made of aluminum, have strong images and colors printed on them, often identifying familiar brands, which can have a reassuring effect. It is simple to convert a drink can into a plant container by removing the top, but beware of the danger of sharp edges. (For advice on dealing with sharp edges, see page 28.) The cans look great on tables and the tops of walls, and are particularly appropriate in a garden that is used for parties and barbecues.

OPPOSITE PAGE, ABOVE **Some junk is already just the right shape for a planter.** For example, these green-painted metal florist's buckets are delightful containers for zantedeschia. The gentle green leaves appear to be natural extensions of the pot, and the flowers create a perfect balance.

OPPOSITE PAGE, BELOW **Extendable flue piping,** which was bought new from a hardware store, serves as an inexpensive pot cover for small plants and lasts well in the garden.

LEFT **A simple coat of paint on a plain tomato can** makes an unassuming junk planter. The wire duck helps to highlight the ribbing on the can.

ABOVE **The ajuga foliage—** which has a dark, slightly metallic hue—sets off this old can without dominating it.

BELOW Junk containers from an earlier period in history can have a powerful effect in a garden, particularly if you take care not to hide their evocative features. Each of these cans tells a different landscape story, and the verbena picks up the background color without competing with it.

RIGHT This exquisite tin cup has a certain air of importance about it, but I wonder if Queen Victoria is entirely happy sitting on a drain cover.

OPPOSITE PAGE, ABOVE LEFT A treasure of a can introduces associations with water. Such discoveries usually fit very comfortably into a garden, and here the foliage of a hebe

splashes over the side of the aquarium, creating a miniature junk story.

OPPOSITE PAGE, ABOVE RIGHT The plaid cookie box has such a powerful color that the bright red geranium almost chose itself. Using complementary colors is often a good idea if you want the junk planter to be a team player.

OPPOSITE PAGE, BELOW Kitchen departments and the kitchen itself are wonderful sources for the best metal junk. This brand-new cake box was inexpensive, and associates well with edibles. The variegated golden thyme works well with the silver sheen of the metal and has a delicious lemon scent.

Pictorial cans add nostalgia.

More flexible are larger cans with pictures of produce on them. Olive containers from Greece, Spain, and France seem to grow in my garden, mingling with cans that once held Polish pickles, Italian tomatoes, or delicacies from Turkey.

Metal containers that were once used to transport and store foods from around the globe give a new meaning to the idea of an international garden; each in its own way conjures up magic from its country of origin. The variety and quality of such cans mean that you are likely to find some that will fit well into your garden. They are still unmistakably metal, even though none of the raw metal actually shows through at first. Weathering ultimately results in that lovely mixture of color, print, bare metal, and rust that reminds me of the kind of balcony garden often seen in Spain or Italy.

One problem with some of these metal containers is that the opening at the top is smaller than the body. Although it is easy to remove the top with a hacksaw, I prefer to keep them intact and to plant young bedding or vegetables in them. A tomato or cucumber that likes plenty of water benefits from having less of its soil exposed to the air because it helps minimize evaporation from the top of the pot. At the end of the season, an old bread knife can be used to chop up the root so you can empty the container to replant it.

Older food cans—often beautiful objects in themselves—can be found in thrift stores and markets. The best are those with lettering or decoration printed directly onto the metal, and they should be treated with some care. Older pictorial cans can add nostalgia to a scene, reinforcing the potential of junk to

conjure up memories and create atmospheres. Certain cans are capable of evoking an era. Some are restrained and understated; others are jazzy, confident, and powerful; even old brand names can conjure up happy memories.

Hinged lids can be valuable as an additional foil for flowers and foliage. Planting a delicate plant in a can with a hinged lid conveys the impression that the plant is regarded as a treasured possession. Alternatively, by a putting a colorful plant in a can with a lid, you can create a jack-in-the-box surprise in a visually quieter area of the garden. Learning to use the garden as a stage and the junk as players is part of the theatrical fun of gardening with planted junk.

The kitchen also provides other, sometimes surprising junk opportunities. A stylish Italian cafetière can be used as a clearly defined temporary home for a plant—clearly defined

Learn to use the garden as a stage —while the junk planters are merely players.

ABOVE **Teapots carry strong associations of relaxing after work or having a break, so they help reinforce one of the main joys of a garden. If you have a big blowsy pot like this one, it's fine to exaggerate its look with a contrasting plant such as a nicotiana.**

RIGHT **When choosing planters for a location with a particular style, such as this modern patio, try something bold like these coffeepots. They fit in well with the alfresco theme.**

OPPOSITE PAGE,
CLOCKWISE FROM TOP LEFT
Enamel teapots are hard-wearing and are made in a variety of valuable colors. This cool blue is rather an unusual color for a garden but it associates well with the gray surface. In a stand-alone container like this, the vivid begonia works well.

An enamel kettle that was no longer needed in the kitchen introduces a unique color scheme to the garden. To make the most of such a scheme, choose a planting that reflects the white-speckled navy blue. Purple-leafed basil and purple sage work a treat.

After I ruined this kettle, it became a lovely junk planter. The combination of red with the oranges of the calendula, partly hidden by the ivy, is both showy and discreet.

An old teapot casts an attractive shadow on a latticed table.

A copper kettle is a simple way to bring a beautiful material into the garden.

The brown and toffee-colored pansies give the impression of coffee flowing out. You can almost smell the strong aroma.

because, however you look at it, it will always be a coffeepot, whereas a tin can, once the label has worn away, can take on an air of anonymity. Planting a former coffeepot with a coffee-colored plant will create the sort of rhythm that can be so rewarding with good planted junk. In this case, the combination can act like a jolt of caffeine.

Pitchers, particularly a matching family, can be ideal junk planters. A group in a variety of sizes can be arranged to resemble a line of ducks and ducklings marching through the flowerbed. A harmonious selection of metal kettles or teapots—which are rarely used in the kitchen these days—can look restful and well coordinated when they are placed in a line, partly owing to the strong association between a refreshing cup of tea and a break in a working day. Try to achieve consistency in a planting of this kind, to knit the group together.

Enameled pots make fascinating bases
for different flower and leaf shades.

LEFT These enamel pitchers and pots, planted with an echeveria, a sedum and a festuca, help integrate the house and garden and look gorgeous in themselves.

ABOVE LEFT Attractive on account of its shape and color, this metal pitcher is made even more eye-catching by the words printed on it.

ABOVE The foliage color of this purple-leafed smokebush is powerfully set off by the dark casserole pot. The slate mulch helps define the top and creates a screen for the shadows.

ABOVE CENTER Combining an edible such as this olive tree with a food storage container creates a simple junk story.

ABOVE RIGHT The shape of this water bowl makes it a valuable container for shallow-rooting plants. The metal stand links it firmly with the ground.

Enameled pots make fascinating bases
for different flower and leaf shades.

Metal cooking equipment is valuable to the junk gardener. Saucepans of all shapes and sizes, from a small poacher to a large cauldron, can be used. Going through my own cabinets was a revealing experience, because there were a quite a few pans that had not seen a flame for at least five years. But beware: an ugly pot will make an ugly planter, and saucepans with long handles can be difficult to incorporate in a garden because they take up a lot of room and do not add much to the scene.

Old cake pans are both stylish and practical as planters. They look very effective when they are planted up with herbs—another variation on the food theme. New cake pans can also be used to produce interesting results. With new shiny metal objects such as these, consider using plants with variegated leaves to mirror the bright reflections in the metal.

Temporary containers, such as foil trays for takeout food, are useful as temporary homes for plants. However, their lack of rigidity means that these planters can easily get squashed out of shape when full of soil, particularly after a downpour.

Enameled pots and objects are extremely powerful and unusual in both texture and colors, providing fascinating bases for different flower and leaf shades. They can also work well in situations where the predominant features are sharp edges and water. There are some exquisite enameled pieces that need minimal planting to look wonderful.

Metal drawers and trays are convenient shapes for junk planters. Shallow ones make great temporary display homes for flowering plants, and older ones are suitable for some of the old-fashioned plants, such as *Primula auricula* or Sweet William. This puts the spotlight on another junk "story": old-fashioned plants in old junk can take us back to a different era.

Filing-cabinet drawers are also a practical shape, but tend to sit uneasily in a garden. They are a reminder of work and, unlike smaller drawers, likely to be difficult to disguise. Many people find paperwork and filing among the dullest, most irritating jobs in the world, so why have any reminders of them in your garden?

Galvanized metal is all the rage in the garden. Handsome but expensive galvanized containers have been specially manufactured for growing plants. Junk solutions can provide imaginative additions or substitutions for these. For example, a galvanized kitchen waste can makes an elegant container, and if it is on wheels it has the advantage of being easy to move. Unfortunately, the more traditional galvanized version, often converted into a garden incinerator, is inextricably linked with

A purple-leafed euphorbia with lime-green flowers looks comfortably at home amid the ivy. If the euphorbia had been planted in a bed, the ivy would have swamped it within weeks, so the galvanized bucket not only looks fabulous, but also provides a home for a plant combination that would not have been possible without it. The wall bracket helps to integrate the wall with the ground.

The intricate detail on this coal-scuttle hinge and the container's weathered surface highlight the attractions of making planters out of items that would more usually be found indoors.

You can introduce height into a bed by using an upside-down trash can and a metal junk planter. I really like doing this because it raises the beautiful pansies to a level where they can be better appreciated. The mass planting of one color is extremely effective.

The splashes of paint that are visible on these galvanized buckets suggest the wonderful process of aging that I am so keen to see in a garden. The pale pink primroses create harmony and need no other colors to interfere.

These metal buckets are among those unused objects that benefit from being given a new role in the garden. They work especially well in a mixed area, and the tomatoes will thrive. Try to keep the metal in the shade to prevent the roots from frying.

Primula auricula and other primroses are grouped together in the shade. Still in their terracotta pots, the primroses have been placed in a metal sifter that offers good drainage and unifies the scene culturally and esthetically.

OPPOSITE PAGE, ABOVE LEFT **This mysterious tub is an old pressure cooker whose geometric quality makes it suitable for a site with dominant architectural elements and straight lines. The weathering of the metal suggests the effects of water.**

OPPOSITE PAGE, BELOW LEFT **A stainless steel asparagus steamer has a beautiful reflective quality in a position dominated by stone.**

OPPOSITE PAGE, RIGHT **The brown-red foliage of a bronze fennel fits well in an old filing drawer.**

A deep bucket is an ideal shape.

trash and can look uncomfortable in many gardens settings. But in a backyard, where real trash cans can be seen, a galvanized version used as a planter can aid the transition between the house and the back door.

Old dishwashing and laundry basins, many of which are enamel, make relatively wide and shallow junk planters, and are excellent for floral and bedding displays. Deep galvanized buckets make an important contribution to planted junk because the shape is horticulturally ideal, with a good root-holding capacity to surface area. Many small shrubs and herbaceous plants grow happily in them, and they fit into many different styles of garden.

BELOW LEFT **When a corner of your yard is dominated by such a chunky structure as this metal water tank, metal planted junk can introduce a more appropriate horticultural theme, helping integrate the structure into the wider garden scene. The pinks of the** petunias, spirea, and geraniums also soften the whole picture.

BELOW CENTER **A strange hot-water boiler, slightly obscured by tall-stemmed foliage and planted with golden-leaved lysimachia, brings a quirky element to the flowerbed.**

BELOW RIGHT **The coal bucket is made to look more natural at the edge of the bed by adding to it the same mulch as that used on the neighboring path. I like this method of taking an unusual object and thinking of imaginative ways to establish it in a garden setting.**

They are also great to use as temporary plant holders and as part of the garden "gallery" because they are easy to move, and most have handles—so it seems natural to move them once in a while. When you are hunting for junk, you may discover, as I did, some curious sources of containers. An army surplus store had good-value old buckets, as well as a lot of other desirable (and not so desirable) objects.

One of the most appropriate junk-metal objects for a garden is the galvanized watering can. Although it would be dishonest to suggest that most people are likely to have one in the garden, I have managed to find them in secondhand stores, with holes in the bases. They are much better value when they can no longer do the job they were made for; and if they

ABOVE **The clematis flowers tumbling nonchalantly out of this green watering can appear beautiful and delicate against a metal background. A vigorous plant like this must be kept well fed and watered to continue to thrive.**

BELOW **Familiar garden tools and equipment make an easy transition to planted junk. It is no surprise to see a watering can and a wheelbarrow in a garden setting, even though they are no longer doing the jobs they were designed for.**

OPPOSITE PAGE **Artistic license has transformed an ordinary watering can into an inanimate and very stylish zebra. The variegated coronilla picks up on the striations, while the cat clearly believes that it has found its cousin.**

A watering can
fits naturally
into the scene.

already have holes it means you won't have to drill them. A watering can fits naturally into a garden scene, but the planting space within it is limited compared with the can's bulk, so I like to plant a container like this with something that rambles around it and eventually up its spout. A watering can also looks at home against a background of plants, particularly when placed in a perennial bed containing old favorites such as delphiniums and lupines.

Wheelbarrows similarly fit naturally into the garden scene, and because of their size, they can be used for mass plantings of slightly larger plants. One of the advantages of older gardening equipment is that it is often nice and rusty, having spent many years in the open air.

FAR LEFT Wonderful shadows are cast by this old birdcage against the mellow decay of an old cookie box. The variegated coronilla has just the right amount of sparkle in its leaf to complete the display.

LEFT AND BELOW In a narrow garden these slender containers made of discarded corrugated iron are stylish in themselves and attractive around plants.

A little bit of rust, gradually spreading into a soft russeting, is part of the natural process of aging.

BELOW A metal pan has become a delicate planter filled with mint and a ranunculus. The mint will eventually swamp everything else, but will not become a pest, as it would in a flowerbed.

BOTTOM A rusty cookie box overflowing with lemon-scented variegated thyme conjures up a delicious taste as well as a lovely picture. It deserves a special place in the garden.

Other rusty items deserve a place all of their own. Rust that appears on machines, cars, or objects in the house is often seen as the enemy, but in the garden a really rusty can looks as if it belongs there—it almost appears to be growing out of the soil and at the same time decaying into it.

The garden is a favorable environment for rust because it is constantly being exposed to moisture whether it rains or not. Rust in the garden can best be appreciated in the fall because its color harmonizes with the bronze-tinted sun, the autumnal browns and reds, the leaf fall and the subsequent decay of the leaves. There can be poetry in a picture.

Even corrugated iron makes a fabulous junk planter when it is rusty. One of the marvels of this kind of gardening is that a material commonly associated with a degree of dereliction can create the opposite impression—one of regeneration, like nature returning—when used well and sparingly. I have seen corrugated iron being used to create raised beds that are effectively giant junk planters with no bases.

The opportunity to recycle materials is an added bonus for the junk gardener. I enjoy the idea of a material like corrugated iron, which is usually regarded as ugly, having a role to play in the creation of something as beautiful as a garden.

Hoppers can sometimes be found in dumpsters.

Hardware stores are one of the unexpected purveyors of junk planters—and the plumbing section can be especially fruitful. Water pipes are available in all shapes and sizes, and brand-new ones can look stylish, particularly near water in a setting with strong architectural features. I am not sure how the merchant would respond to gardeners coming in to buy pots—it might be wise not to seek any gardening advice. As any dumpster-holic will tell you, old pipes are easy to find, and even the beautiful hoppers used to cap old drainpipes—real junk treasures—are often thrown away.

OPPOSITE PAGE, LEFT **What could be more appropriate as an adornment for a roof garden than these old drain hoppers? It is surprising that they can be found in dumpsters. If you come across one, attach it to a wall and plant it. Creating a natural setting for a junk planter gives the scene a certain rhythm, which is much more restful to live with than shocking contrasts. The trailing** ivy-leafed geraniums will grow to create a tumbling pink cushion; they are easy to look after and reasonably drought-tolerant.

OPPOSITE PAGE, RIGHT **A** weathered white hopper lies casually beside a crocus display set just below a window. Some planted junk works well simply placed in close proximity to unplanted pieces.

RIGHT **Aluminum pipes that make sleek, stylish, and good-value planters can be found at hardware stores, which are generally excellent sources of junk containers.**

BELOW **Not an everyday find, a lead pump with missing handle fits neatly into a corner of the garden, flanked by interesting containers and plants, and requires minimal planting.**

Water pipes come in all shapes and sizes

The delicacy of wirework suggests that each piece has been individually hand-crafted.

ABOVE LEFT **Wirework has a delicate quality and—even in an urban location—brings a country feel to a garden. It may be its link with craftsmanship that gives this material a sense of timelessness, as though each piece had been carefully handmade. The primroses are apparently being nurtured in the wire basket.**

TOP **A dried-flower head imaginatively placed in a wirework basket creates a delicate picture based on harmonious patterns. Junk containers do not always need to be full of plants to look good in a garden.**

ABOVE **Simple wirework makes a temporary home for plants.**

ABOVE RIGHT The shapes of some of your junk finds will suggest where in the garden they should be positioned. Many wire spheres began life either as egg baskets or as the frames of the paper lampshades that were ubiquitous in the 1970s (though these cannot take much weight). These objects were made to hang, so putting them into trees shows them off to best advantage.

ABOVE, FAR RIGHT A more suitable wire container takes the form of a common garden object. Here a growing bean plant has been offered protection from slugs and snails—though, knowing how extremely cunning and persistent these creatures are, I wouldn't be surprised if they managed to climb up and slide in, and be delighted to have found such a good food cage.

BELOW RIGHT I repeatedly warn people to avoid the wrong associations when they introduce planted junk into a garden. Even though I think most garbage cans are a bit trashy with plants, this is something of a gem from the 1960s that makes a good junk planter. Luckily the dwarf hebe is not sulking about the fact that its new home had such an unsavory past.

BELOW, FAR RIGHT Flowers can really pick up on the strengths of junk. In this example, whirly-petaled African daisies have a delicacy that is similar to the narrow-gauge wire used to create the wirework patterns.

Some of the more delicate metal junk planters are made of wirework—the simplest and least attractive being shopping baskets, which can be serviceable as homes for new plants before they are permanently planted. More elaborate old-fashioned wirework looks wonderful against a beautiful background such as an old wall. Sympathetically planted and surrounded by other delicate objects, wirework can help to create a warm country picture.

Quirky objects have impact because of their capacity to surprise, and toy trucks that have been planted with a seasonal display can bring a childlike joy to people of all ages.

ABOVE LEFT **The Coca-Cola label introduces a touch of color and a sense of lightheartedness to a garden.**

ABOVE RIGHT **You may have guessed that I like having fun in the garden. Life can become very serious at times, so combining a bit of playfulness with childhood memories—evoked in this case by a colorful old toy—can bring an entirely new dimension to your outside space.**

OPPOSITE PAGE, ABOVE LEFT **A toy crane stands guard over a calendula in a nesting kettle.**

OPPOSITE PAGE, ABOVE RIGHT **The Swan River daisy thrives as nature returns, swamping another crane near the old industrial area by my pond.**

OPPOSITE PAGE, BELOW **Truckloads of flowers process in stately fashion along a narrow road. The bright colors pick up the dominant color of the wall.**

If you have an adventurous personality, junk planting offers boundless opportunities to indulge your gardening fantasies. You will find that some quirky objects can be great fun in a garden setting. Toy trucks and cranes are particularly wonderful, and my big sulk came when someone snapped up the metal truck that would have fitted perfectly with my cranes around the pond. Planted with a seasonal display, these trucks can bring a childlike joy to people of any age.

Quirky does not have to mean weird. A metal trunk is a lucky find and can become a focal point in a display. By contrast, there are more challenging planters, such as the former army helmet I once found, that create a reflective mood, evoking thoughts of a garden of remembrance. These feelings are not new in a garden; historically, some gardens were seen as spiritual places, capable of both uplifting and saddening the soul. The individual took a journey through the garden, and each feeling was confined to a separate area and a separate view. It would be rare to have space for such a journey in a small garden, where it is more important that the main views do not try to encompass too many different moods and styles. In some small gardens you can create different areas so the whole garden is not revealed at once— which gives you the opportunity to be more playful with junk.

plastic and rubber

Plastic may not be the first type of material that you think of when considering how to introduce planted junk into your garden. The idea of plastic among the plants seems at first rather tacky—and, admittedly, the wrong piece of plastic junk in a garden can look dreadful. On the other hand, a well-chosen and well-used plastic junk planter can look marvelous. In the case of plastic, there is not much space between attractive and ugly. What's good is great, but what's bad is awful.

Children will be familiar with the more accessible plastic junk planters used for germination, such as empty yogurt cups and plastic party cups. Small pots full of germinating seeds can introduce a sense of nurturing to an area of the garden, in that they are devoted to raising young plants for the future.

At school we used to germinate seeds in empty yogurt cups—and they do the job well.

Water bottles of all sizes make surprisingly stylish addition to the junk planter repertoire. The various brands of bottled water are differentiated by the shapes, designs, and colors of the bottles, and some of the bottles are quite sleek. Water has an easy and comfortable association with the garden, so the bottles do not look out of place.

By cutting a bottle in half and using the top half as the plant pot and the bottom half as a saucer and a stabilizer, you have a container with a ready-made drainage hole and water reservoir. The bottles are great for bedding plants and herbs, and the slightly tinted ones prevent roots from being scorched

OPPOSITE PAGE, ABOVE **This plastic Greek olive barrel (empty, unfortunately) had been thrown out by a food importer. A few holes drilled into the base made it into a large junk planter ideal for seasonal bedding.**

OPPOSITE PAGE, BELOW **If you buy manure in a bucket as a fertilizer, like this poultry manure, there is no longer any need to throw out your empties.**

BELOW **Recycling water bottles is valuable from both an ecological and horticultural point of view. Here the bottles are used as early-season cloches for edibles, to help protect young cut-and-come-again lettuces from slugs, snails, and late frost. They look charming and surprisingly professional.**

RIGHT **A discarded kitchen cabinet and some yogurt cups looks as if they were created to live near the ocean. The color scheme of white and shades of blue is reflected in the planting of polemonium (Jacob's ladder) and scaevola. This arrangement has been designed to harmonize with the beauty of the place rather than to challenge it.**

ABOVE **The late 1950s are revisited in this combination of a polka-dot display and a table from that era. The re-creation of an earlier period of history is something that we are used to seeing indoors, but it is rarely attempted in** the garden. There is no point in trying to be subtle when planting such bold pots.

OPPOSITE PAGE, ABOVE **Most** everyday plastic objects are made in fairly gaudy colors, as if the makers are seeking to show off the versatility of the material. This allows great freedom in choosing plants to put in them. But plastic is also a very powerful material in terms of its effect on the rest of the garden, so it must be introduced with discretion.

OPPOSITE PAGE, BELOW, LEFT AND RIGHT **Many plastic planters that you are likely to find are hard to take too seriously, so enjoy them. This planted toy truck is fun, and the bright pink who-knows-what has at last found a useful role in life.**

by the sun. I tend to keep any clear-plastic bottles I have planted in a slightly shady place, and I love to see the roots explore the insides of the containers as the plants grow. The bottles also make excellent cloches to go over young plants that need to be hardened off in early spring, and to help to protect plants from slugs and snails. The larger flagon types are particularly useful for this.

There are plenty of other drinks bottles and liquid storage bottles that have potential as junk containers, but the branding on them is important—bleach containers, for instance, look completely out of place in a garden. There is something charmingly eccentric about a group of bottles being used as planters.

Plastic teacups and glasses (perhaps from a picnic set) usually come in gaudy colors, showing just how versatile plastic can be. Make good use of the strengths of such items; they can generate both a powerful nostalgia and liveliness in an already colorful garden. Planted junk should always be chosen to harmonize with its setting: those same cups would look out

Some of the jazzy colors perform with real star quality in the right setting.

of place in a formal garden dominated by shades of green, but some of the jazzy colors demonstrate star quality in the right environment. Small plastic toys, particularly watering cans, can be amusing props in the garden. Mingling with small plants and other plastic junk, they can contribute to the creation of a

rather delicate miniature world. Plastic buckets have a special place in many people's memories because they are reminiscent of childhood vacations at the beach. If you love the ocean but live miles away from it, you can capture the beach nostalgia by establishing an area of sand, bleached wood, and little plastic buckets. If you are lucky enough to live near the ocean, buckets are a must. Even though most of them come in hideous colors, it doesn't appear to matter. There is no point in trying to be subtle when planting up a plastic bucket—you'll fail.

Larger plastic buckets have virtually no associations with the beach. What was nostalgic and fun where a small bucket was concerned takes on a much more serious image when a large bucket appears. Larger buckets brings to mind mops or dishcloths and plastic gloves: housework is the order of the day. However, some garden fertilizers are sold in plastic buckets, and they have altogether different connotations, to do with fertility and feeding the soil.

Some foods are transported to wholesalers in bulk in large plastic barrels. These barrels represent excellent value and can be incredibly useful in the garden; there are few large junk containers that last as well as these or hold as much soil. They are also easy to transport when empty and not at all fragile. I have used large blue plastic barrels for growing zucchini,

Create an area of sand, bleached wood, and **planted plastic buckets.**

OPPOSITE PAGE, TOP **The bedding plants appear to be bright and chirpy in their bright and chirpy new home.**

OPPOSITE PAGE, CENTER **A yellow bucket associates well with water and looks quite at home among the yellow water irises and filled with a yellow calla lily.**

OPPOSITE PAGE, BOTTOM **Old weathered buckets—a satisfying dumpster find—are a convenient size for plants. These hebes seem to pour out of them in a very colorful way.**

LEFT AND BELOW **Some objects seem to transform themselves effortlessly into planters as soon as they become plant homes. However, these plastic buckets will always look like plastic buckets, so there is no point in trying to disguise them. This flowering maple (abutilon) with its bright-red flower seems to be the perfect match for the red buckets. The handles make the buckets easy to move for changing displays.**

BELOW **Old plastic baskets that were once used for laundry or shopping can serve a useful purpose if you have a nursery area in your garden. The yellow chrysanthemums look appealing while they are waiting for a more permanent position.**

BELOW RIGHT **With a little imagination, junk can be used to help display plants at various different levels in a garden. This trash basket gives height to a seasonal display and creates an intricate and unusual foil for low-growing alpine penstemons.**

which have performed well and look stylish with their yellow trumpet flowers standing out from the powerful blue. Barrels can also look marvelous overflowing with flowers. Less attractive ones can be used to give height to low-growing plants; stand them in a bed behind other plants so the barrel disappears and only the plant is visible.

Barrels are available from some food-processing factories, or from food stores with a fast turnover. The managers of the factory near my home were absolutely delighted when I turned up to take some barrels because I saved them having to pay for disposal.

Drinks crates can be used to stand plants in, and if they are put in the right place, particularly near a door, they welcome you into the garden when you leave the house and welcome you back home on your return. This is another example of using unexpected objects in a familiar way, so that the display doesn't look out of place. Planting colorful flowers is effective because the flowers appear to be glad to see you.

Finer plastic mesh baskets—from colanders to wide-meshed laundry baskets—are useful for standing other pots in. Some plants continue to

Colorful flowers are rewarding because they appear to be glad to see you.

BELOW LEFT **Shallow plastic objects such as these colanders are easy to use in a bed, and are not too showy when placed amid plants. The pansies benefit from being slightly raised and having a splash of blue plastic visible, while the sedum looks as if it is melting into the alchemilla and over the edge of the red plastic container.**

BELOW **Sometimes after a trip to the garden center it takes a while to get round to planting your new acquisition. This soon-to-be-planted columbine has been temporarily displayed in a plastic mesh wastebasket. Such a basket seems less incongruous than many other trash cans do in the garden.**

The brash colors of a group
of plastic baskets can have a
joyful effect when the baskets
are full of bright little plants.

thrive when they are planted directly into containers with smaller holes, but it is advisable to keep the body of the container out of the sun to prevent the plant's roots from becoming scorched.

There are plenty of small plastic baskets that can be tremendously enjoyable to play with in the garden, particularly for cameo displays. Some of them are difficult to imagine on their own in any garden, but the brash colors of a group of baskets can be a joyful sight when filled with bright little plants. This is the least serious part of being a junk gardener: trying things that may only be used for a week or two.

The plastic bags used for fertilizers and soil can make useful containers, but they have a limited life because the sun tends to degrade the bags, and the plastic becomes brittle and breaks. They do not look out of place in an informal garden because they are horticultural in origin, and they

LEFT, TOP TO BOTTOM
The bright tropical colors that adorn this bowl are complemented by a startled pink geranium to generate a lively Mexican feel.

Little plastic bags such as these are difficult to take very seriously, but they can have a genuinely useful role in the garden as temporary plant holders. I doubt that Gertrude Jekyll would have approved, but the petunia looks happy enough with its surroundings – although it will need to be transplanted soon.

The pastel shades of this plastic shopping bag do not transform it into something subtle. It remains a bag, but conjures up relaxing thoughts in my mind—reminders of preparing to go to the beach— so it can be quite a calming object to have around at the end of a hard day.

A rather lovely large laundry bag looks perfectly at home among a clump of mauve flowering erysimum. The colors are attractive together and, thank goodness, aren't a reminder of doing the washing.

OPPOSITE PAGE, ABOVE, LEFT AND RIGHT **The succulent spiny leaves of a lotus interrupt the reflective shine of glossy colored plastic.**

OPPOSITE PAGE, BELOW RIGHT
These African daisies, born in a nursery and sold at a garden center, have only one more trip to make before finding their permanent home in a bed.

OPPOSITE PAGE, BELOW FAR RIGHT
Junk time-travel can take you back to your favorite era in the privacy of your own yard. Here the destination is the 1960s.

THIS PAGE **Part of my junk journey has been to discover that tires can fit into the garden without making it look like a scrapyard. Painted tires can bring an element of fun into a garden. They are a great shape, fit well into a flowerbed, and survive through all weathers. It is also better for the environment than destroying them.**

ABOVE LEFT **Contrasting colors—such as this trailing blue lobelia in a pink tire—can create a spectacular display.**

BELOW LEFT **This would be a special bed with or without the tires. But they add definition and contrast, and I particularly like the translucent reds of the beefsteak plant (iresine), which gives the impression of being a foliage extension of the rubber.**

TOP RIGHT **The joyous greeting given by the dwarf sunflowers (helianthus) in a pale blue tire could not be farther from the traffic jams and exhaust fumes that the tire is more usually associated with. What a great reincarnation.**

CENTER RIGHT **For clumsy plants such as petunias, a tire can make a good rim to tumble over.**

BOTTOM RIGHT **A diascia, another attractive and long-flowering trailer, is about to launch itself over the side.**

OPPOSITE PAGE, ABOVE AND BELOW **These tires were bought as plant pots, having been recycled and remolded for that purpose. They look stylish and have no feeling of the scrapyard or abandoned vehicles—particularly when used in this vertical arrangement on a ladder. In a display like this, which relies on a repeated use of the same container, use the same plant in each to increase the impact of the whole display.**

Boldly painted tires introduce an element of fun into a garden.

are a convenient size for larger plants. In the good old days, nurseries used them to grow plants to a specimen size; in my nursery I have grown strawberry trees more than six feet tall in old fertilizer bags.

Another synthetic material worth considering is rubber. Tires in a garden look unpleasant when misused or misplaced, and may make the garden resemble a scrapyard, but they can provide a useful raised area, and a coat of paint can lift them so they become a rather nice home for bedding plants or, as we found out, a great plaything for kids. There are now some containers for plants made out of recycled tires, and these are both stylish and ecologically sound.

Although some of the containers described in this chapter really do push out the boundaries of taste, plastic junk can go farther than most in the weirdness stakes. I once planted a large bright yellow wastebasket and tried to find the right place for it; eventually it settled in a bed where it was completely hidden by shrubs. I am sure that there is a garden somewhere out there crying out for a large splash of yellow plastic—but it simply isn't mine. However, some of the quirky plastics, such as brightly colored hardhats and large plastic funnels, can look spectacular, and some of the really cheap storage containers are a great size for many plants.

Recycling tires, rather than discarding them, is good for the environment.

mixing materials

Most new junk gardeners start by mixing their newly acquired treasures with other, more traditional pots that have already found a place on the patio or in the beds. Gardening with junk is not an exclusive style that makes conventional pots redundant. Indeed, some of the finest displays I have seen consist of an eclectic mix held together by compatibility.

I use containers as if they were plants, experimenting with shapes and colors to achieve a display that looks good. Often it just involves a bit of trial and error—sometimes simply swapping positions can help. Above all, don't worry: no display will ever be perfect.

As the first few planted junk displays are introduced into your garden, other opportunities will present themselves, and various containers, both traditional and junk, can become an integral part of the picture. I still find myself acquiring beautiful terracotta pots to fit in with the cans, boxes, and bowls that adorn my garden.

The materials naturally occurring in any garden scene are incredibly varied, which means that being restrictive is less natural. The house is likely to have, at the very least, glass windows, walls of wood or brick, and plastic drainpipes, while

Some of the finest displays I have seen are a completely eclectic mixture.

OPPOSITE PAGE **A mixed bed characterized by plenty of horticultural variety provides the opportunity to create an illusion that the planted junk is itself part of the planting. The combination of different materials is quite appropriate in such a setting. In a natural flowing bed such as this, use materials and colors that are themselves natural. The bed is the star of the show and should not be upstaged.**

ABOVE **This collection of planted junk helps to create height and interest in a space under a tree when the ground cover needs a bit of spicing up. The bed itself is full of tree roots, so the containers are really valuable.**

LEFT **Wicker and metal make a happy partnership in a planting of herbs and flowers. Allowing the viewer to enjoy only a hint of the metal bucket is a very effective use of the planter.**

the garden often has fences, soil, plants—and a sky ranging from shades of blue to puffy white and threatening grays. Trying to achieve a uniform style of pots, plants, and design would be quite a task when everything else is so diverse. A mixture of containers is simply an extension of the mixture that already exists. In my garden a rusty old tin can sits happily near bleached wood and a chipped ceramic pot, with a terracotta Ali Baba jar making a contented neighbor, whatever the weather. However, a shiny galvanized metal container looks out of place with the rusty can because it clashes with the theme of natural aging.

In a garden dominated by mixed beds, using a variety of containers can look as natural as using a variety of plants. In a bed that relies on the flow and movement created by plant associations, where the shapes of individual groups of plants create a rhythm of curves, use containers that fit in with the flower and foliage colors, favoring those made from natural

Choose pots that complement the flower and foliage colors.

materials that age well, such as metal, wood, and terracotta. Much of the beauty of gardens that use plants as a framework derives from the fact that there are few hard surfaces on view; most of the walls are hidden. When using containers in beds you can adopt the same approach by concealing part of the container—to give the impression that it is planted in the bed itself—and letting the plants dominate.

Where there are hard surfaces on view you can afford to be bolder and use larger containers, which help create a coherent scene. I use the top of my brick wall as well as the bed as a stage for planted junk, and the mixture of materials, shapes, and levels seems to integrate the ground with the sky.

In a garden that is already well filled with pots, planted junk can fit in and enhance the display. Again, there are already so many textures and materials on view that adding junk does not necessarily challenge the eye.

So many gardens are already mixing materials in a creative way, from stone and little rocks to wood and terracotta, that it would almost be more unnatural to restrict the planted junk materials too much. This bag of citrus fits into the garden quite happily, especially because the citrus theme is continued in the terracotta pot.

A setting like this, which is so charmingly chaotic and informal, is a marvellous place for all sorts of junk containers. The bleached gray of the wood is beautiful, and suggests that brightly colored junk would be too visually greedy.

Although stone and wicker are very different materials, the similar patterns help to link the containers.

This cat cast himself in the role of sceptical observer of the scene.

This tableau encompasses a mixture of materials, colors, and textures, and yet it works wonderfully well as a coherent whole. The grouping of wire, metal, ceramic, painted and terracotta pots is completely in keeping with the rather romantic background of the mounds of plants, particularly the contrasting textures of the ferns and the hosta.

Unexpected combinations of the eccentric and the traditional can be the basis of a strongly integrated display.

It is the overall effect of introducing junk containers that matters, so don't be afraid to experiment. Anything too eccentric may seem visually greedy, however, and can shift the focal point of the scene, upstaging the other containers. Using foliage and flowers that look good together is as important as the choice of container. Repeated use of a family or even a variety of plants contributes to a strongly integrated display.

In some gardens or areas traditional containers appear more eccentric or out of place than junk pots. This effect can commonly be seen near an old shed or storage area whose contents are often on view through the window and where some tools never make it inside. The result is often a bizarre jumble of images—from lawn mower and empty wheelbarrow to compost heap and bags of fertilizer. Strange combinations of the eccentric and traditional can help to tie the scene together.

Modern minimalist gardens are more restrictive in style, and—although mixing up styles and materials can work well— you need to choose containers that enhance the clean, sharp lines. In some of these gardens the plants tend to be well controlled and static, resembling architectural structures. Use pots that also remain consistent—for instance, galvanized metal ones that do not age or decay.

Formal gardens rely on a degree of symmetry and control, and generally need classical containers with simple shapes. There is no problem about mixing different styles of container

OPPOSITE PAGE **A mixture of metal and plastic beach buckets filled with brightly colored bedding plants highlights the beauty of this beach scene. I cannot think of a more desirable view to have from my window.**

BELOW **These junk containers have found a quiet and sheltered corner of the garden in which to congregate. Although not all shy and retiring, they are restrained enough to form a harmonious association with the silvered wood. The effect is enhanced by the silver-leaf peperomia planted in the metal sifter.**

UPPER ROW **Details of the main photographs, or variations on them, highlight the harmonies of texture and color that can be achieved in this style of gardening.**

LOWER ROW, LEFT **Items that pose as junk are sometimes not really junk at all. It would be galling to be told that you could pick up a piece as stunning as this angel statue in a scrapyard. In fact, the statue was left in the garden by a previous owner, and probably originally belonged in a church. I like the association between the strong reds of the nasturtium (tropaeolum) and the monkey flower (mimulus) in the pot on the pedestal. The variously shaped terracotta pots are in keeping with the whole scene.**

LOWER ROW, CENTER **Some junk can be incredibly useful in the garden for purposes other than planting. This old hospital cart has been put to good use in the area of a community garden where the hard work is done. It is movable, useful for storage, and ideal as a potting bench. It resembles a really well-designed bit of garden equipment, and— along with the yellow bucket, which is being used to soak dry plants—shows the potential versatility of junk in the garden. If it were placed in a bed, the cart would remind me too strongly of a hospital, so I like to keep it around at the back.**

LOWER ROW, RIGHT **A charmingly eclectic wall scene incorporates pieces of junk that not only provide homes for plants, but also combine to create a picture that is powerfully evocative of the countryside. The little wall cabinet resembles a miniature reflection of the complete arrangement.**

OPPOSITE PAGE **The powerful and dominant colors and images in this garden make an inviting stage for some well-chosen junk. The bright colors of some of these junk planters appear to be in keeping with the whole garden. They enhance existing elements rather than competing with them—while pastel colors might have looked out of place. Junk stories are fun and bring a new dimension to gardening. Scenes such as the one with the guitar, though unbelievably contrived, can stimulate the imagination. Whom does the hat belong to? Do they play country and western or blues? Are they going somewhere? The velvety claret of a salpiglossis looks moody in the leather hat.**

Brushstrokes
from a few
junk planters
offset strong
color
schemes.

RIGHT **The combination of a red begonia in a red oriental vase, a white miniature rose in a rubber container, and an oriental umbrella demonstrates how few rules there are.**

FAR RIGHT **A successful way to integrate different types of junk planter is to fill them with the same variety of plant. This establishes consistency, as exemplified by these metal and ceramic junk planters linked by lavender.**

in a formal garden, but introducing too many images confuses the eye, and there is a danger of undermining the simplicity of the formal effect. Choose plants that pick up the formality of the rest of the garden, and consider introducing topiary balls or pyramids, which can look great.

Gardens with a dominant color or color scheme in the bed or on the walls can benefit from the brushstrokes of a few junk pots and the broader sweeps of mixed displays. It is helpful to put the pots in place and step back to inspect them from the main viewing points, then move them if necessary.

This highlights one of the liberating aspects of any kind of container gardening: you can move the containers at any time of year. I have a whole host of pots that are well-seasoned travelers, having taken short vacations under the bamboo, stayed for a couple of weeks near the Ali Baba jar, and even spent a while in the water. The tomato plant in the paprika can has moved from a position close to the house in early season—where it is well protected when the weather is cool—to the end of the garden in

midsummer to catch the sun, and then to the shade of the north wall when I was away from home for a while. A citrus fruit in an old metal can from France finds itself just beside the window when it is flowering, so it is in the right place at the right time for me to enjoy its scent.

Not all junk containers will look attractive in your garden. Occasionally I have come home victorious with a dumpster trophy, grinning at my own cleverness, only to skulk out a week later with the same treasure, now destined for the trash. These are rare events. On the whole, I have found that planted junk has helped create beautiful and interesting gardens without the need to redo everything, to remove what is already there, or to spend a fortune. Above all, creating wonderful displays with a mixture of planted junk is great fun.

Mixing up junk containers in your garden is a liberating experience because it costs little in time or money if you change your mind about the effect you want to achieve.

ABOVE **Planters assembled over the years by a junk collector have been arranged to make an informal garden even more lovely. The mixture of materials and styles feels natural, where a more rigid styling would seem completely out of place.**

LEFT **Terracotta mingles with kettles, teapots, pitchers, chairs, and lots more in this junk pot bed. Pots are planted to look exuberant, and the flowering specimens can be moved to the front and then moved back after flowering. This marvelous versatility is one reason why I love container gardening.**

OPPOSITE PAGE **A variety of images from the same garden conveys the impression that complete freedom has been exercised in the choice of containers—even though there is consistency in the color and aging of the junk and the pots. The silvery gray of the old wicker, the partly bleached wood of the barrel, and the worn white chair all contribute to the sense of charming and manageable decay. The metal fluted container is so at home that it looks like an extension of the clapboarding. Such harmony makes for a relaxed and gentle atmosphere.**

Here are some of my favorite plants for planted junk. The main criteria for inclusion are that they thrive in containers, look good for a long time, and are easy to look after, but this list is by no means comprehensive, and I advise everyone to experiment and have fun. For simplicity, I have given the genus or the species of each plant, followed where appropriate by its common name. Where applicable and useful, plant hardiness zones are also included.

PART THREE

plant directory

Zones are based on the average annual minimum temperature for each zone; the smaller number indicates the northernmost zone a plant can survive in; the higher number the southernmost zone the plant will tolerate.

KEY

H Height S Spread Z Zone

Z1:	below -50°F (-45°C)
Z2:	-50° to -40°F (-45° to -40°C)
Z3:	-40° to -30°F (-40° to -34°C)
Z4:	-30° to -20°F (-34° to -29°C)
Z5:	-20° to -10°F (-29° to -23°C)
Z6:	-10° to 0°F (-23° to -18°C)
Z7:	0° to 10°F (-18° to -12°C)
Z8:	10° to 20°F (-12° to -7°C)
Z9:	20° to 30°F (-7° to -1°C)
Z10:	30° to 40°F (-1° to 4°C)
Z11:	above 40°F (4°C)

BEGONIA

DIMORPHOTHECA

FELICIA

PRIMULA

GAZANIA

annuals

Ageratum FLOSS FLOWER

H: 6-12in (15-30cm) S: 8in (20cm)

Blue, white, or pink powdery flowers. The blues are rather artificial-looking and need careful partnering. Choose dwarf varieties.

Alyssum

H&S: 3-6in (7-15cm)

Tiny mounds of slightly honey-scented pink or white flowers. Alyssum overflowing the edges of a container is reminiscent of a frothy drink.

Antirrhinum SNAPDRAGON

H: 6-20in (15-50cm) S: 4-16in (10-40cm)

Vast color range, including wonderful red-browns. Choose dwarf varieties.

Arctotis AFRICAN DAISY

H: 6-12in (15-30cm) S: 10in (25cm)

Showy daisylike flowers, opening in sun and closing when dull. Great in shallow containers with a limited volume of soil.

Argyranthemum MARGARITA

H&S: 12-36in (30-90cm)

Half hardy. Daisylike flowers and ferny foliage. Lots of colors, including pink and yellow. Water generously in summer.

Asteriscus

H: 8-12in (20-30cm) S: 12in (30cm)

Half hardy. Forms a spreading mound with bright yellow flowers in summer. Good for container edges.

Begonia

H: 6-12in (15-30cm) S: 12in (30cm)

A useful foliage and flowering plant, particularly for shade.

Brachycome SWAN RIVER DAISY

H: 18in (45cm) S: 16in (40cm)

Bluish-purple or white daisylike flowers above downy gray-green leaves. Water generously for a long display.

Calendula POT MARIGOLD

H: 12-24in (30-60cm) S: 12-18in (30-45cm)

Profusion of orange or yellow daisylike single or double flowers from midsummer. Slightly scented leaves. Deadhead regularly to achieve a succession of flowers.

Coleus

H: 6-18in (15-45cm) S: 12in (30cm)

The bright red, green, and creamy yellow leaves of coleus were staples of Victorian bedding displays, but are only recently back in vogue. Pinch out tips to keep plants bushy.

Dahlia

H: 12-24in (30-60cm) S: 18in (45cm)

Bold splashes of color from midsummer, ranging from white to yellows, oranges, and reds: singles, doubles and pompoms. Choose the smaller bedding varieties.

Dianthus CARNATION, PINK

H: 6-12in (15-60cm) S: 8-16in (20-40cm)

Flowers may be single, double or ruffled, in shades from white to deep red. Deeply scented hardy varieties provide a nostalgic scent in early summer.

Dimorphotheca AFRICAN DAISY

H: 8-18in (20-45cm) S: 6-12in (15-30cm)

Half-hardy free-flowering white or purple daisy. Excellent for shallow pots. Some forms overwinter in containers in well-drained soil.

Felicia BLUE OR KINGFISHER DAISY

H&S: 12-18in (30-45cm)

Bushy plants produce mass of daisylike bright blue flowerheads with yellow centers. Good in mixed plantings or in the front of a container.

Fuchsia

H&S: 12-24in (30-60cm)

Single or double tubular or bell-shaped flowers range from white through reds to purple. Upright, bushy, or trailing types.

Gazania SOUTH AFRICAN DAISY

H: 10-16in (25-40cm) S: 12-24in (30-60cm)

Reliable exuberant daisies with deep-yellow centers and petals in reds, oranges, and yellows, some striped. Plant for showy brilliance in full sun; the flowers close in dull weather.

Glechoma GROUND IVY

H: 16in (5cm) S: 36in (90cm)

Green kidney-shaped leaves edged and marbled in white. One of the best foliage plants for trailing over the front of a container.

Helichrysum

H: 12-36in (30-90cm) S: 36in (90cm)

Half hardy. Another foliage plant, with small felted leaves: usually silvery gray, but can be golden or variegated. Mound-forming or trailing varieties.

TAGETES

VIOLA

Impatiens BUSY LIZZIE

H&S: 6-16in (15-40cm)

Brightly colored flowers and fleshy foliage. New Guinea group have abundant pink, red, lavender, and white flowers all summer, with beautifully variegated leaves. Great in shade.

Lantana

H: 12-30in (30-75cm) S: 36in (90cm)

Verbenalike flowers may be cream, pink, orange, yellow, or a mixture. Ideal for growing through other plants or at the front of a tall or hanging container. Aromatic leaves.

Lathyrus SWEET PEA

H: 6in-7ft (15cm-2m) S: 6in (15cm)

Let tall sweet peas climb up supports in a big container. Old-fashioned varieties are best for scent; modern ones have larger, more striking flowers in virtually any color except yellow.

Lobelia

H: 4-6in (10-15cm) S: 6-16in (15-40cm)

Traditional favorite for container edges. Bright blue or white lobelia will flower all summer, as long as it doesn't dry out.

Lotus CORAL GEM, PARROT'S BEAK

H: 8in (20cm) S: 12-24in (30-60cm)

Orange-red to scarlet flowers that resemble parrots' beaks appear in summer among silvery needlelike leaves on trailing stems.

Mesembryanthemum LIVINGSTONE DAISY

H: 4-6in (10-15cm) S: to 18in (45cm)

Large, brightly colored, daisylike flowers form a gaudy carpet in a sunny summer. Good for shallow containers.

Myosotis FORGET-ME-NOT

H&S: 6-18in (15-45cm)

Plant with bulbs for late spring color. The smaller pink forms tend to be less reliable than the traditional taller blue varieties. Looks messy after flowering, so transfer to a bed in summer, where it may self-seed.

Nemesia

H: 6-10in (15-25cm) S: 6in (15cm)

The lower and upper lips of these trumpet-shaped flowers are often of contrasting colors. Flowers may be marked or edged in another color. They make attractive early-flowering indoor plants in colors from white through blues to pinks, reds, and oranges.

Nicotiana TOBACCO PLANT

H: 12-48in (30-120cm) S: 12-24in (30-60cm)

Modern dwarf varieties are especially popular for containers because they are erect and open-faced, but tall old-fashioned varieties have superb evening scent and are good for larger containers near windows.

Pelargonium GERANIUM

H: 6-18in (15-45cm) S: 6-10in (15-25cm)

A single-colored upright plant; a lax cut-leaved variety; single or double blooms, compact or spreading: there are pelargoniums to satisfy all tastes. Deadhead regularly for continuous flowering, and water well during a hot summer.

Petunia

H: 6-18in (15-45cm) S: 12-36in (30-90cm)

Irresistible splashes of color all summer. Grow in a sheltered spot and deadhead frequently for a long flowering period.

Primula POLYANTHUS, PRIMROSE

H: 6-14in (15-35cm) S: 4-16in (10-40cm)

Many varieties; reliable spring color, but may need protection from birds. Can be planted out in a shady spot after flowering.

Scaevola

H: 4-6in (10-15cm) S: 12in (30 cm)

Intensely blue flower with petals on one side only. Good trailer that loves sun.

Tagetes AFRICAN MARIGOLD, FRENCH MARIGOLD

H: 8-16in (20-40cm) S: 12-18in (30-45cm)

Open-faced, single, double, or tightly curled pompoms; marigolds thrive in pots to provide lasting color and excellent cut flowers.

Tropaeolum NASTURTIUM

H: 6-36in (15-90cm) S: 6-18in (15-45cm)

Climbers, trailers or mound-forming plants in all shades of red, yellow, and orange, plain or with cream stripes, some with speckled leaves.

Verbena

H: 6-18in (15-45cm) S: 12-20in (30-50cm)

Clusters of cream, peach, and all shades of pink to purple flowers appear at the end of long stems. Ideal for trailing or in a mixed planting. All are long-flowering, but become shy in cool spells.

Viola PANSY

H&S: 6-10in (15-25cm)

Good for cooler gardens. Can flower for up to five months in the right conditions, even in winter. Summer-flowering varieties are also good for semishady situations.

CROCUS

MUSCARI

NARCISSUS

bulbs

Anemone blanda

H: 5in (12cm) Z: 4-8

Plant in September for very early spring display. Colors include white, shades of blue, pink, and bright red. It also has an attractive cut leaf.

Convallaria LILY OF THE VALLEY

H&S: 4-6in (10-15cm) Z: 2-9

Scented flowers and rather lovely, even when only in leaf. The white form is the strongest. Can thrive in shade.

Crocosmia MONTBRETIA

H&S: 18-24in (45-60cm) Z: 5-9

Straplike leaves and long stems covered in small trumpet flowers from mid to late summer. Some stunning colors, such as the burnt-orange 'Emily McKenzie.'

Crocus

H: 3-4in (7-10cm) Z: 3-9

Huge range of colors. Crocuses are delicate and beautiful, but flower for only a short time and are vulnerable to being flattened by early spring downpours.

Galanthus

H: 4in (10cm) Z: 4-8

The common snowdrop, *G. nivalis*, is a wonderful, easy-to-grow bulb that is able to thrive in the shade.

Lilium LILY

H: 12-39in (30-100cm) S: 8-12in (20-30cm)

There is something magnificent about a lily in a container. Try some of the compact scented varieties such as 'Mr Ruud', or, if you have enough space and a large enough pot, the dizzy-making scent of 'Stargazer' is hard to beat. There are almost too many wonderful lilies, and part of the fun is choosing them. They enjoy well-drained soil.

Muscari GRAPE HYACINTH

H: 6in (15cm) Z: 4-8

Easy to grow and can tolerate shade. Looks particularly effective when mass-planted in a shallow container, even when only in bud. Plant in early fall.

Narcissus DAFFODIL

H: 4-12in (10-30cm) Z: 4-9

'Tête à Tête' is still one of the best and longest lasting varieties of daffodil for a container. Otherwise, choose from the many dwarf varieties or from the early-flowering *cyclamineus* group. Many of the delicate jonquilla type are scented.

Tulipa TULIP

H: 6-12in (15-30cm) Z: 5-9

Tulips planted in a group look glorious in pots. The range is enormous. Good choices for containers include the smaller species such as *T. greigii* through to the slightly taller, salmon-pink 'Clara Butt'.

edibles & herbs

Basil

H&S: 8-16in (20-40cm)

The small-leaved Greek basil is well suited to growing in a small container, while the leggier sweet Italian basil has a better taste. Try growing basil near tomatoes. The purple form is more difficult to grow.

Beans, dwarf French

H&S: 12-18in (30-45cm)

These have delicate flowers and delicious pods. They can be trained into a spiral for a satisfying visual effect. The purple-podded varieties look wonderful.

Beans, runner

H: up to 10ft (3m) S: 12in (30cm)

Grow in a large container up wires or a tepee. They look spectacular mixed with morning glory. Red, white, or bicolored flowers over a long period, in addition to an abundance of succulent beans.

Chives

H&S: 8-10in (20-25cm) Z: 3-9

Easy perennial that is capable of doing well in the sun or shade. The delicate foliage tastes at its strongest before the attractive pink flowers start to show.

Cucumber

H: 59-71in (150-180cm) S: 20in (50cm)

A surprisingly easy variety to cultivate is 'Crystal Apple,' which has a profusion of small yellow fruits following bright yellow flowers. These cucumbers have a deliciously crunchy taste.

Eggplant

H: 12-30in (30-75cm) S: 10-24in (25-60cm)

With its attractive felty leaves and small pale-purple flowers, eggplant looks particularly good on a sunny windowsill inside or outside the house. There are many unusual varieties to experiment with.

Fennel

H: 48in (120cm) S: 24in (60cm)

Hazy feathery foliage and flat heads of yellow flowers create a soft effect in any garden. Great in a movable container because it makes a wonderful foil for other plants.

Lettuce

H&S: 8in (20cm)

Choose the cut-and-come-again varieties, such as lollo rosso, which can be picked over a long period.

Mint

H&S: 12in (30cm) Z: 5-9

A surprisingly varied species. Many mints are excellent, if invasive, container plants. Great in any conditions. The ordinary garden mint is one of the best.

Parsley

H&S: 10in (25cm)

Curly-leafed parsley looks much more decorative in a pot than the flat-leafed variety. Prefers rich soil. Don't let it dry out.

Peppers

H&S: 12-18in (30-45cm)

Huge range now available. The hotter the pepper, the more sun it needs. The compact varieties look attractive in fruit, particularly in a red fire-bucket.

Rosemary

H&S: 8-39in (20-100cm) Z: 8-10

Many forms, from the spreading 'Severn Sea' to 'Miss Jessopp's Upright.' All are evergreen and fragrant with beautiful flowers. Grow in a sunny position; avoid winter waterlogging. Tends to live for only about five years.

Sage

H&S: 12-24in (30-60cm) Z: 3-10

Attractive shrub with a choice of leaf colors. The lovely purple-leafed form prefers sun and good drainage. Sage has a limited life.

Strawberry

H: 6in (15cm) S: 12in (30cm)

Strawberries thrive in pots, and their delicious fruits fill the air with a sweet scent. They will tumble over the sides of your junk planter and be slightly protected from slugs.

Thyme

H: 2-12in (5-30cm) S: 6-12in (15-30cm)

Useful evergreen spreading herb. Delicious to use, attractive in leaf and when flowering. Best in sun and well drained. The ornamental variegated thyme is lemon-scented.

Tomato

H&S: from 12in (30cm)

Easy to grow in containers, with an enormous variety of types, habits, and fruits. Keep well fed and regularly watered.

Zucchini

H: 12-20in (30-50cm) S: 24in (60cm) & more

Fantastic in a pot in a small garden with lots of rich composted soil and well watered. Majestic large leaves and bright yellow flowers. Trailing varieties can be over 6ft (2m) long.

BASIL

LETTUCE

SAGE

THYME

TOMATO

CYCAS REVOLUTA

DRYOPTERIS AFFINIS 'CRISTATA'

OSMUNDA REGALIS AND SCOLOPENDRIUM

CORDYLINE AUSTRALIS

ferns, grasses, & palms

Brahea armata BLUE HESPER PALM

H: 39in (100cm) S: 24in (60cm)

One of the world's bluest palms; requires sun and shelter. Plant in well-drained soil, water well in summer and keep dry in winter.

Cordyline australis CABBAGE PALM

H: to 72in (180cm) S: to 36in (90cm) Z: 9-10

A good plant to have on its own in a pot. The purple form is less hardy than the green.

Cycas revoluta JAPANESE SAGO PALM

H&S: 36in (90cm)

Uniquely prehistoric-looking. Hardy in warmer climates, but worth bringing indoors in winter.

Dryopteris

H&S: 24in (60cm)

Large fern family, including the evergreen *D. erythrosora* (**Z: 5-8**) with bronze-red young leaves and the common male fern *D. filix-mas*, (**Z: 4-8**), which is an elegant and adaptable plant for sheltered shade.

Festuca glauca BLUE FESCUE, GRAY FESCUE

H&S: 12in (30cm) Z: 4-8

Lovely evergreen grass with bluish-gray foliage and feathery flowers. 'Elijah Blue' is a reliable strain. 'Golden Toupee' has fine golden foliage.

Hakonechloa macra 'Aureola'

H&S: 10in (25cm) Z: 5-8

A delicate-looking plant with golden arching foliage that waves gently in the breeze. Dies back in winter.

Ophiopogon planiscapus 'Nigrescens'

H&S: 4in (10cm) Z: 5-8

This extraordinary black grass is an excellent ground cover. Can be painfully slow to grow.

Osmunda regalis ROYAL FERN

H: 39in (100cm) S: 24in (60cm) Z: 4-9

A large handsome fern that needs moist conditions, so keep it in some shade.

Phyllostachys

H: to 10ft (3m) S: 24in-7ft (60cm-2m)

P. aurea (**Z: 5-10**) is an outstanding bamboo with golden stems. *P. nigra* (**Z: 7-10**) has fine foliage and a stunning black stem. Both grow tall, but do well in large pots. Bamboos thrive in sun or shade, but become very thirsty, especially in sunny and windy positions.

Pleioblastus

H: 36in-10ft (90cm-3m) S: 20-48in (50-120cm) Z: 5-10

Smaller varieties of this bamboo grow well in containers. *P. auricomus* is a variegated form with yellow stripes in the leaves.

Polystichum setiferum SOFT-SHIELD FERN

H&S: 24-36in (60-90cm) Z: 5-8

Evergreen and elegant. The soft-shield fern keeps its gloss through most of the season and grows in dry shade.

Trachycarpus fortunei

H: to 10ft (3m) S: 36in (90cm) Z: 7-10

Evergreen hardy palm with majestic fanlike leaves borne on a thick hairy trunk. Needs good drainage.

HAKONECHLOA MACRA 'AUREOLA'

BRAHEA ARMATA

ARUNDINARIA AURICOMA

OPHIOPOGON PLANISCAPUS 'NIGRESCENS'

perennials & shrubs

Acer MAPLE

H: to 7ft (2m) S: 20in (50cm) & more Z: 5-8

Any smaller-growing variety is suitable for a container; the best are Japanese maples with divided leaves and bright autumn colors. Place in a cool semishady place.

Agapanthus AFRICAN LILY

H: 10-30in (25-75cm) S: 16in (40cm) Z: 7-10

Wonderful, almost spherical flowers held well above the straplike foliage. The colors range from intense blues to almost pure white. Excellent in containers in bright sun.

Ajuga BUGLEWEED

H: 4in (10cm) S: 12in (30cm) Z: 3-9

Semi-evergreen that thrives in the sun or shade. Blue flowers in summer are held above leaves that vary from green and cream to bronze and brown.

Alchemilla LADY'S MANTLE

H&S 8-16in (20-40cm) Z 3-7

A. mollis has pale-green wavy-edged foliage and greenish-yellow flowers. Great partner to many plants. Thrives in sun or shade.

Armeria THRIFT

H: 4-12in (10-30cm) S: to 12in (30cm) Z: 4-8

Deep green cushions of tightly packed lance-shaped leaves sprout tall stems with spherical alliumlike red, white, or pink heads in early summer. The neat clumps are great in small pots and give the sense of being near the sea.

Buxus BOX

H: from 10in (25cm) S: from 8in (20cm) Z: 6-8

B. sempervirens is an adaptable evergreen that is perfect for clipping and shaping into topiary specimens; usually seen as balls or pyramids. *B. suffruticosa* is the slow-growing fine-leafed variety.

Camellia

H&S: 24-36in (60-90cm) Z: 7-9

The flowers bring brightness to a garden in winter, and the glossy evergreen leaves make an excellent summer background when other plants are in bloom. Good in shade; avoid early morning sun when in bud. Plant in a soil mix for acid-loving plants.

Campanula BELLFLOWER

H: 4-10in (10-25cm) S: to 24in (60cm) Z: 4-8

While most bellflowers are upright, the trailing forms work well in containers and tumble and spread with abandon.

Choisya MEXICAN ORANGE BLOSSOM

H&S: to 48in (120cm) Z: 7-9

Heavily scented white starry flowers are produced abundantly over glossy green foliage in late spring. The neat rounded evergreen bushes are great for a dull corner. The golden form is slow-growing, and the cut-leafed 'Aztec Pearl' doesn't appreciate root restriction.

Clematis

H: up to 13ft (4m) Z: 4-9

The most suitable varieties are the smaller-flowering species such as *C. macropetala* and *C. alpina*, but some of the larger-flowering varieties can spice up a display, provided that they are planted out in the garden after they flower. Keep sun off the roots.

Convolvulus cneorum

H: 12in (30cm) S: 18in (45cm)

A delicate silver-leafed ground-cover plant that has trumpet-shaped white flowers through summer. It is evergreen and likes a sunny position. Needs really good drainage, particularly in winter.

Cotoneaster

H&S: to 59in (150cm) Z: 6-8

Choose a compact mound-forming or prostrate variety to provide ground cover. Bears inconspicuous white flowers in summer and berries in the fall. Can brighten a damp shady winter garden where little else is able to flourish.

Daphne odora 'Aureo-marginata'

H&S: 18in (45cm)

An evergreen slow-growing shrub with delicately gold-margined leaves. Needs some shelter from cold winds. The pink flowers from late winter to early spring are among the most exquisitely scented in the garden. A gem.

Euphorbia SPURGE

H&S: 12-36in (30-90cm) Z: 5-9

Mostly evergreen. Gray fleshy leaves and extraordinary green flowers in spring. The ground-covering *E. robbiae* is capable of growing in the deepest shade, and the purple foliage of *E. amygdaloides* 'Purpurea' is unique. Can cause skin rash.

Ficus FIG

H&S: 24in (60cm) to huge Z: 8-11

Figs like their roots confined, so they do well in containers. Place in as sunny a position as possible. The leaves are majestic and aromatic, and the fruits are delicious.

AJUGA PURPURESCENS

CLEMATIS MACROPETALA

EUPHORBIA AMYGDALOIDES 'PURPUREA'

HELLEBORUS ORIENTALIS

HOSTA SIEBOLDIANA

PRIMULA VIALII

Fuchsia

**H: 24-59in (60-150cm) S: to 36in (90cm)
Z: 7-9**

A wide variety of perennial fuchsias, with
many different flower styles and colors, is
available for permanent planting . My favorite
is the white form of *F. magellanica,* which also
has a fascinating peeling bark.

Geranium CRANESBILL

**H: 8-16in (20-40cm) S: 12in (30cm) and more
Z: 4-9**

The true geranium is a spreading perennial
with a range of cut-leafed foliage and
beautiful flowers. Some geraniums, such as
the *G. macrorrhizum* varieties, are semi-
evergreen. They creep over the sides of
containers, and gently soften the edges.

Hebe

H&S: 6-48in (15-120cm) Z: 7-9

Family of neat evergreen plants producing
spikes or small heads of flowers in blue,
white, pink, red, and purple. Some have
variegated foliage. The hardiest are the
smaller-leaved varieties.

Helleborus CHRISTMAS ROSE, LENTEN ROSE

H&S: 12-18in (30-45cm)

Great for color in winter and early spring.
H. niger (**Z: 4-7**)is ideal in the shade, and looks
best where it can be seen from the house. The
flowers of *H. orientalis* (**Z: 5-9**) come in a
variety of delicate shades. Grow in large
containers, and keep well fed.

Hosta PLANTAIN LILY

H&S: 8-39in (20cm-1m) Z: 3-9

Ideal for containers, especially if slugs are
a problem. Wide range of clump-forming
plants grown principally for their mounds
of overlapping heart-shaped to lance-shaped
leaves. Colors range from silvery-blue to lime
green splashed with cream. Keep moist and
grow in a shady place.

Hydrangea

H&S: 36-48in (90-120cm) Z: 6-9

Large spherical mopheads or flat lacecaps
of flowers that continue through summer.
H. petiolaris, the climbing hydrangea, has
lacecap white flowers and a peeling bark.
An excellent plant for shade.

Iris

H&S: 12-36in (30-90 cm) Z: 4-9

Irises do well in containers. They vary from
the narrow-leaved *I. sibirica* to the dwarf
winter-flowering *I. stylosa.* Their flowering
period is not particularly long, so they
should be grown as much for their foliage
effect as for the beauty of their blooms.

Lavandula LAVENDER

H&S: 12-36in (30-90cm) Z: 5-8

All lavenders can thrive in pots well mulched
with sand, and will flower through summer.
The dwarf *L. angustifolia* 'Hidcote' and
L. angustifolia 'Munstead' are the strongest
colors. In cooler areas you can grow more
tender French lavender varieties in pots,
move them into the sun in the summer
and overwinter them indoors.

Papaver nudicaule ICELANDIC POPPY

H&S: 8-12in (20-30cm) Z: 2-7

The Icelandic poppy comes in many colors
and, although it is short-lived, can make
a marvellous display in a pot.

Phormium NEW ZEALAND FLAX

**H: 36-64in (90-160cm) S: 36in (90cm)
Z: 8-10**

The tall swordlike leaves may have pink
or brown margins or centers as well as the
hardiest all-green variety. To encourage
growth, lift, divide, and repot every couple
of years in spring.

Pinus PINE

H: to 7ft (2m) S: 36in (90cm) Z: 2-9

Choose a dwarf or prostrate variety and
plant in a large pot so it will not need to
be repotted; pines do not like to have their
roots disturbed. There are suitable blue,
gray-green, and dark-green varieties.

Pittosporum

H: to 7ft (2m) S: to 60in (150cm) Z: 8-10

Bushy evergreen shrub with crinkle-edged
leaves and black young stems. Leaf colors
include purple, and silver-edged green, as
well as dark green. *P. tenuifolium* and its
varieties are the best for containers, although
in protected gardens *P. tobira* does well, too.
Not for very exposed gardens.

Primula PRIMROSE

H: 2-6in (5-15cm) S: 6in (15cm)

A varied and valuable group of plants for spring color. *P. auricula* (**Z: 3-7**) can be stunning; some are fully hardy, many appreciate some protection in winter.

Rhododendron

H: 12-60in (30-150cm) S: to 51in (130cm)

Compact varieties make excellent long-lasting container plants. *R. yakushimanum* (**Z: 4-7**) has a gray dusting on its leaves and wonderful flowers. Grow in sun or semishade and keep well watered. Plant in a soil mix for acid-loving plants.

Rosa

H&S: vast range

Choose smaller-growing scented varieties, particularly from the patio or groundcover range. Most roses prefer sun.

Saxifraga SAXIFRAGE

H: 2-6in (5-15cm) S: to 12in (30cm)

Leafy cushions sprout upright stalks topped with loose clusters of starry flowers predominantly in pinks, reds, and whites.

Dozens of varieties range from tiny and compact to more untidy forms.

Sedum STONECROP

H: 2-4in (5-10cm) S: 4-12in (10-30cm)

Sedum is a very easy plant to grow in containers because it is drought-resistant and maintenance-free. Produces a mass of starry flowers above a dense mat of succulent leaves, often tinged with reds or yellow.

Sempervivum HENS-AND-CHICKS

H: 2-6in (5-15cm) S: 2-4in (5-10cm) Z: 4-9

Most successful when grown in gritty soil, houseleeks send up thick stalks with pink or red flowers above rosettes of fleshy leaves. They need minimal care. Varieties with red or green leaves are most reliable outdoors; those with felty or hairy leaves need to be kept dry during winter.

Vinca PERIWINKLE

H: 4-12in (10-30cm) S: 12in (30cm)

The starry blue flowers of this evergreen are perhaps best seen trailing from a container; the plants are invasive in open ground. Variegated-leaved forms do not flower as freely as those with plain dark-green leaves.

Wisteria

H: 17ft (5m) and more S: 24in (60cm) Z: 5-9

Traditionally grown against the wall of a house, where soil may quickly become dry and impoverished, wisteria is often just as happy growing in a large tub of rich soil. Grow as a small standard, on a wall, or over an arch, where the long chains of white, pink, or lilac flowers have space to fall.

Yucca

H&S: 18-30in (45-100cm)

Magnificent evergreen with swordlike leaves and huge plumes of white bell flowers in late summer. *Y. filamentosa* (**Z 4-10**) is slow-growing and free-flowering, while *Y. gloriosa* is more architectural. Yuccas all prefer sun and very well drained soil; move into a more sheltered position in winter.

Zantedeschia ARUM LILY

H&S: to 36in (90cm) S: 24in (60cm) Z: 8-10

The arum lily is one of the most elegant of all plants when grown alone in a container. Erect white funnel-shaped flowers create an illusion of splashes of light springing out of dark green or white-splashed leaves. Keep moist and well mulched.

PRIMULA AURICULA

SEDUM

where to find pots

Thrift stores, dumpsters, and garage sales are among the good sources of junk planters, but some salvage yards and domestic hardware stores are also worth trying.

Ace Hardware Corporation
2200 Kensington Ct.
Oak Brook, IL 60523-2100
(630) 990-6600
www.acehardware.com
Hardware from A to Z. Plenty of seasonal gardening supplies.

Architectural Salvage Warehouse
53 Main Street
Burlington, VT 05401
(802) 658-5011
www.architecturalsalvagevt.com
Strange and wonderful, urns, fixtures and relics—all salvaged from residences and buildings.

Adkins Architectural Antiques
3515 Fannin St.
Houston, TX 77004
(800) 522-6547
www.adkinsantiques.com
Salvaged architectural artifacts, including urns and gargoyles.

The Flea Market Guide
www.fleamarketguide.com

Qflea.com
http://www.qflea.com
An online flea market with more than 400 vendors.

The boxLot Company
12526 High Bluff Dr., Suite #250
San Diego, CA 92130
(877) 426-9568
www.boxlot.com
Auction-style website with garden tools, accessories and collectibles.

Brooks Barrel Company
5228 Bucktown Rd.
P.O. Box 1056
Cambridge, MD 21613
(800) 398-2766
Hand-crafted wooden barrels, kegs and planters of all sizes.

Dan's Garden Shop
5821 Woodwinds Circle
Frederick, MD 21703
(301) 662-3572
www.dansgardenshop.com
Good source for plastic pots of all sizes, including bulb pans and plastic "terra cotta."

FrenchWyres
P.O. Box 131655
Tyler, TX 75713
(903) 561-1742
Fanciful wire baskets, troughs, stands and spheres.

Garden.com
www.garden.com
Texas-based supplier of all things gardening, including a diverse selection of planters.

Gardener's Supply Company
128 Intervale Rd.
Burlington, VT 05401
(888) 833-1412

The Home Depot
2455 Paces Ferry Road
Atlanta, GA 30339
(800) 430-3376
www.homedepot.com
Chain store with home and garden supplies. Good source for annuals in season.

Home Harvest Garden Supply Inc.
3807 Bank Street
Baltimore, MD 21224
(800) 348.4769
www.homeharvest.com
Good selection of items, including plain nursery pots, fiber pots and plastic saucers.

Ikea
(800) 434-IKEA
Simple, inexpensive designs. Lots of storage ideas.

Kinsman Company
River Road
Point Pleasant, PA 18950-0357
(800) 733-4146
www.kinsmangarden.com
Good selection of classy garden items, including moss-lined baskets and troughs.

Kmart
Stores all across the U.S.A.
To find one near you,
call (800) 355-6388
www.kmart.com
Chain store with gardening supplies and seasonal flowers.

Martha By Mail
P.O. Box 60060
Tampa, FL 33660-0060
(800) 950-7130
www.marthabymail.com
Unusual containers and urns.

Simple Gardens
615 Old Cemetery Road
Richmond, VT 05477
(800) 351-2438
www.simplegardens.com
Containers, watering systems, plant stands—especially for gardeners with limited space.

Target Stores
33 South Sixth Street
Minneapolis, MN 55402
(888) 304-4000
www.target.com
Slightly sophisticated plastic.

Walt Nicke's Garden Talk
P.O. Box 433
Topsfield, MA 01983
(978) 887-3388
www.gardentalk.com
Fine tools, garden ornaments.

Windowbox.com
817 San Julian St., Suite 406
Los Angeles, CA 90014
(888) GARDEN-Box
www.windowbox.com
Especially for the rooftop or balcony gardener. Unusual planters and loads of online advice.

where to find plants
Here is a small selection of the many excellent garden centers and nurseries that can be found throughout the U.S.A.

Avant Gardens
710 High Hill Road
North Dartmouth, MA 02747-1363
(508) 998-8819
www.avantgardensNE.com

Annuals, tender perennials and unique tropicals with a special section for container gardening.

Bamboo Sourcery
666 Wagnon Rd.
Sebastopol, CA 95472
(707) 823-5866
www.bamboo.nu
Excellent collection of bamboo-family plants.

The Banana Tree Inc.
715 Northampton St.
Easton, PA 18042
(610) 253-9589
www.banana-tree.com
A fine selection of tropicals, including ginger, bird-of-paradise and, of course, bananas.

Bluestone Perennials
7211 Middle Ridge Road
Madison, OH 44057-3096
(800) 852-5243
www.bluestoneperennials.com
Comprehensive selection of perennials.

W. Atlee Burpee Company
(800) 888-1447
www.burpee.com
A large selection of seeds for flowers and vegetables; some accessories.

The Cook's Garden
P.O. Box 5010
Hodges, SC 29653-5010
(800) 457-9703
www.cooksgarden.com
Flower and vegetable seeds, including many unusual varieties and old-fashioned favorites.

Dutch Gardens
P.O. Box 200
Adelphia, NJ 07710-0200
(800) 818-3861
www.dutchgardens.com
High-quality bulbs from Holland.

Four Winds Growers
P.O. Box 3538
Freemont, CA 94539
(510) 656-2591
www.fourwindsgrowers.com
A good source of dwarf citrus trees: oranges, lemons and others

Glasshouse Works
P.O. Box 97, Church Street
Stewart, OH 45778-0097
(800) 837-2142
www.rareplants.com
Wide range of plants.

Johnny's Selected Seeds
Foss Hill Road
Albion, ME 04910
(207) 437-4301
www.johnnyseeds.com
A huge selection of seeds with an emphasis on heirloom varieties.

Lilypons Water Gardens
6800 Lilypons Lane
P.O. Box 10
Buckeystown, MD 21717
(800) 999-LILY
www.lilypons.com
Water gardening supplies, as well as tropical lilies and lotus that are suitable for containers.

Logee's Greenhouses, Ltd.
141 North Street
Danielson, CT 06239-1939
(888) 330-8038
www.logees.com
A grand selection of tropical and subtropical plants.

McClure & Zimmerman
108 W. Winnebago St.
P.O. Box 368
Friesland, WI 53935-0368
(800) 883-6998
www.mzbulb.com
Huge selection of bulbs, including many diminutive types and tender tropicals.

Select Seeds Antique Flowers
180 Stickney Hill Rd
Union, CT 06076-4617
(860) 684-9310
www.selectseeds.com
Seeds and some plants. A good source for fragrant flowers and many old-fashioned varieties.

Van Bourgondien Bros.
P.O. Box 1000,
Babylon, NY 11702-9004
(800) 622-9997
Bulbs, including dwarf oriental lilies.

index

picture credits

Key: A = ABOVE, B = BELOW,
L = LEFT, R = RIGHT, C = CENTER

FRONT ENDPAPER Thomas Lyttelton's garden in Highgate; 4 Valerie Rossmore's garden in London; 5 AC, AR, & BR the Artist Marilyn Phipps' garden in Kent; 6 B Andrew Harman's garden in London; 7 L Justin De Syllas' house, London; 7 R Belinda Battle's garden in London; 8 A Thomas Lyttelton's garden in Highgate; 9 A Culpeper Community Garden, the Angel, Islington; 9 B Justin De Syllas' house, London; 10 & 11 L Andrew Harman's garden in London; 12 Thomas Lyttelton's garden in Highgate; 13 B & 14 Culpeper Community Garden, the Angel, Islington; 15 L Ros Fairman's garden in London; 15 R Islington Garden designed by Diana Yakeley; 16 L & BR Belinda Battle's garden in London; 16 CR Justin De Syllas' house, London; 18 Ros Fairman's garden in London; 20 R Islington Garden designed by Diana Yakeley; 22 Justin De Syllas' house, London; 23 A Thomas Lyttelton's garden in Highgate; 25 R the Artist Marilyn Phipps' garden in Kent; 36 Helen Pitel's garden in London; 38 Belinda Battle's garden in London; 39 L Islington garden designed by Diana Yakeley; 39 R Belinda Battle's garden in London; 40 AR, 40-41 A & 40-41 B Justin De Syllas' house, London; 40 BL the Artist Marilyn Phipps' garden in Kent; 40 CL Jeremy's garden in De Beauvoir Town, London; 40 BR Belinda Battle's garden in London; 42 Belinda Battle's garden in London; 43 BL Ros Fairman's garden in London; 43 BR Andrew Harman's garden in London; 44 L Belinda Battle's garden in London; 46-47 Justin De Syllas' house, London; 48 Thomas Lyttelton's garden in Highgate; 49 Charles Caplin's garden in London; 51 L Justin De Syllas' house, London; 54 BR Charles Caplin's garden in London; 55 AL the Artist Marilyn Phipps' garden in Kent; 55 AR Belinda Battle's garden in London; 55 BR Culpeper Community Garden, the Angel, Islington; 57 B Ros Fairman's garden in London; 58 L Culpeper' Community Garden, the Angel, Islington; 58 R Ros Fairman's garden in London; 59 L Andrew Harman's garden in London; 59 R Helen Pitel's garden in London;

60 & 61 BL Belinda Battle's garden in London; 61 AR Helen Pitel's garden in London; 62 the Artist Marilyn Phipps' garden in Kent; 63 AR Culpeper Community Garden, the Angel, Islington; 63 BR Karla Newell's garden in Brighton; 66-67 & 68 AL the Artist Marilyn Phipps' garden in Kent; 68 BL Ros Fairman's garden in London; 68 BR Belinda Battle's garden in London; 73 AL the Artist Marilyn Phipps' garden in Kent; 78 A & 79 R Ros Fairman's garden in London; 80 L Culpeper Community Garden, the Angel, Islington; 82 R Justin De Syllas' house, London; 83 AL Valerie Rossmore's garden in London; 84 B & 85 R the Artist Marilyn Phipp's garden in Kent; 85 L & C & 86 B Thomas Lyttelton's garden in Highgate; 87 ACL Ros Fairman's garden in London; 87 BL Helen Pitel's garden in London; 88 AL, BL & 89 C Justin De Syllas' house, London; 88 R & 89 R Thomas Lyttelton's garden in Highgate; 90 Andrew Harman's garden in London; 91 Ros Fairman's garden in London; 92 L Andrew Harman's garden in London; 93 AR the Artist Marilyn Phipps' garden in Kent; 93 BR Ros Fairman's garden in London; 94 L Valerie Rossmore's garden in London; 95 A Justin De Syllas' house, London; 100 AL & BR the Artist Marilyn Phipps' garden in Kent; 100 CR & 101 BR Belinda Battle's garden in London; 100-101 Helen Pitel's garden in London; 101 BL Charles Caplin's garden in London; 103 R the Artist Marilyn Phipps' garden in Kent; 105 A Karla Newell's garden in Brighton; 108 L & 109 R Helen Pitel's garden in London; 111 BL & BR Belinda Battle's garden in London; 112 BL the Artist Marilyn Phipps' garden in Kent; 112 AR Culpeper Community Garden, the Angel, Islington; 113 B Ros Fairman's garden in London; 115 al the Artist Marilyn Phipps' garden in Kent; 115 AR Valerie Rossmore's garden in London; 116 Helen Pitel's garden in London; 117 R Ros Fairman's garden in London; 119 AR Culpeper Community Garden, the Angel, Islington; 120 the Artist Marilyn Phipps' garden in Kent; 122-123 B Culpeper Community Garden, the Angel, Islington; 124 Karla Newell's garden in Brighton; 125 Valerie Rossmore's garden in London; 126-127 the Artist Marilyn Phipps' garden in Kent; BACK ENDPAPER Valerie Rossmore's garden in London.

Organizations whose gardens appear in the photographs:

PAGES 9 A, 13 B & 14, 55 BR, 58 L, 82 R, 88 AL & BL, 89C, 95 A
Culpeper Community Garden
Registered Charity no. 291156

Postal address:
35 Batchelor Street
London N1 0EJ

Site address:
1 Cloudesley Road
London N1 0EG
t. +44 20 7833 3951

PAGES 15 R, 20 R, 39 L
Yakeley Associates Design
Interior and Garden Design
13 College Cross
London N1 1YY
t. +44 20 7609 9846
e. dy@yakeley.com

acknowledgments

Adam Caplin would like to thank all at Ryland Peters & Small, particularly Sailesh Patel for his inspiring design work; Henrietta Heald for her editing expertise, patience and guidance; Alison Starling, Gabriella Le Grazie, Kate Brunt, Sarah Hepworth, Gerald Wratten, Elizabeth of Mar and Joanna Everard for making it such fun to produce the book; Francesca Yorke for her stunning photographs; Rose Hammick for sourcing some real junk gems; Sailesh, Francesca and Rose for their wonderful styling.

Thanks also go to Victoria Robinson for her invaluable help; Sally Bailey of Baileys Home and Garden for some great junk planters; Joe Swift, Sam Joyce and Jo Carey at the Plant Room for their plants and expertise; Ros Watling, Liz Collins and all the team at Whistleberry Nurseries for growing great plants; Islip Street Garden Centre in London and Henry Street in Reading for the loan of plants; Colegrave for their advice; Simon Turner at Twelve mail order for his corrugated-iron pots; Charlie Ryrie for her understanding, Caroline Hutchinson for her patience and support—and all the gardeners listed on page 143 who were generous enough to allow us to invade their space.

Rose Hammick would like to thank the following shops and suppliers for their help in supplying junk containers: Architectural Rescue, CASA, The Old Station, The Junk Shop, Greenwich, SW1 Architectural Salvage, The Odd Shop, Willesden Green Architectural Salvage, Baileys Home and Garden, David Champion, Tobias and The Angel, Bazaar, The Dining Room Shop, Woodpigeon.